THIS BOOK BELO

_____

_____

INTRODUCTION

This How to Draw book is for anyone, whoever you are, artist, beginner or people that love drawing and learning.

Many people think that learning to draw is difficult if not impossible, If would-be artists treated the subject as fun and went about it in the right way, it could be possible for nearly everyone to draw.

This book is all about simplifying things, analyzing them into basic shapes, sketch and link. This book also shows simple step-by-step illustrations for you to follow easily,

BEFORE YOU BEGIN

DRAWING KIT

Having the right tools gives you the determination and courage to be able to create the image you see in your mind and capture that on paper.

Paper

A drawing paper is not only useful for experienced artists but is equally important for beginner artists as well. If you are newbie who has just started drawing for the first time, it is better that you start with a simple pack of printed paper.

Pencils

The first drawing tool that you must use if you have just entered the drawing field is a drawing pencil. They're made of graphite and are graded in soft to hard ranges. In this book, you will need pencils for sketching a lot.

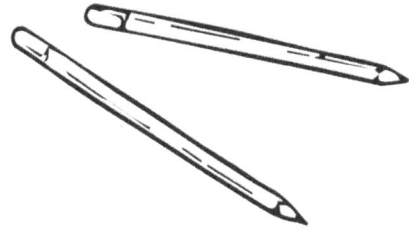

Erasers

Don't be afraid of making mistakes, when you have erasers, if anything gets wrong, it can be corrected easily. They can be shaped to erase precise areas and for "lifting out" highlights in heavy tonal areas.

Sharpening tools

Apart from an eraser, the pencil sharpener is another important tool that you must have while drawing. While using a pencil sharpener, make sure that you get a good quality sharpener with a sharp blade, hence offering you a smooth sharpening experience.

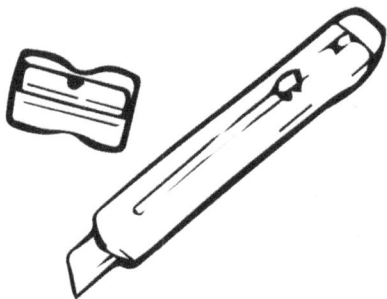

Brush/Ink pens

Like drawing pencils, brushes/ink pens also ncome in various styles; it may be brushed tip pens, square marker pens, hard and round-tipped pens, or fine-tipped pens. Every type of pen is used for a specific purpose.

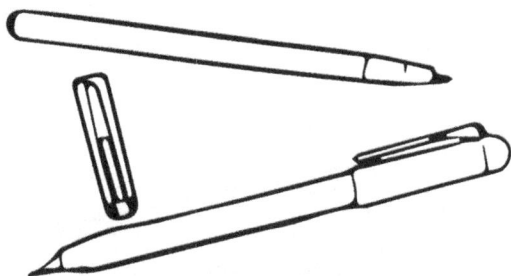

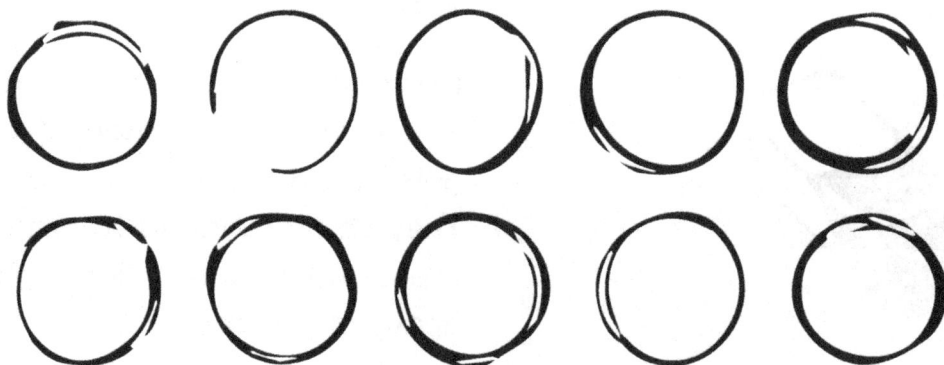

TABLE OF CONTENTS

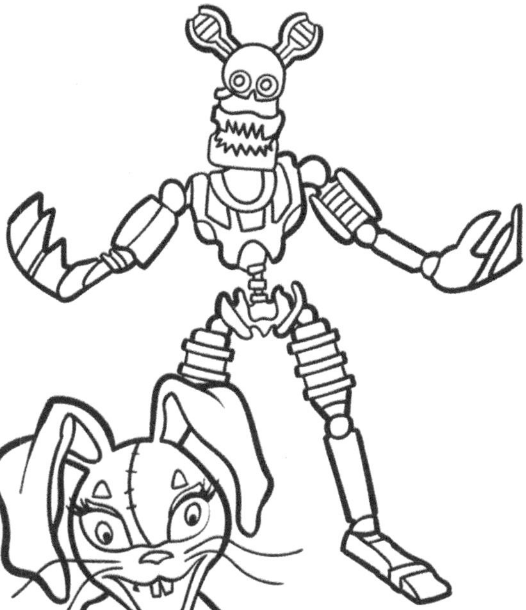

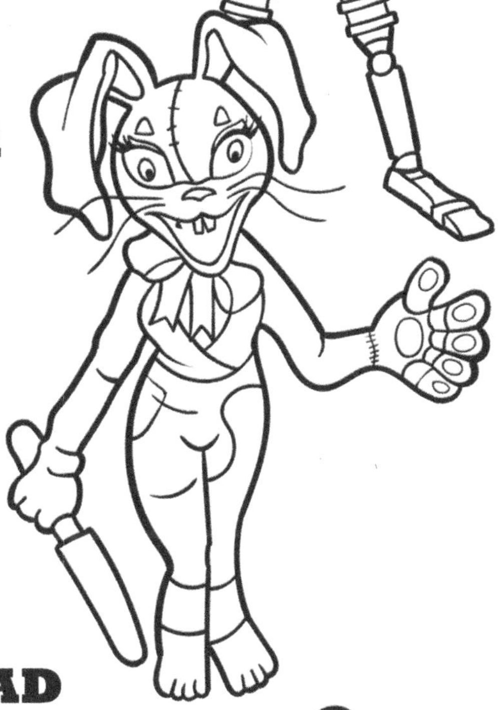

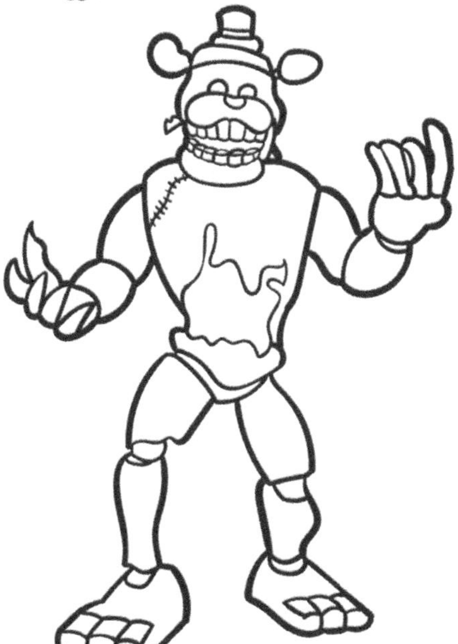

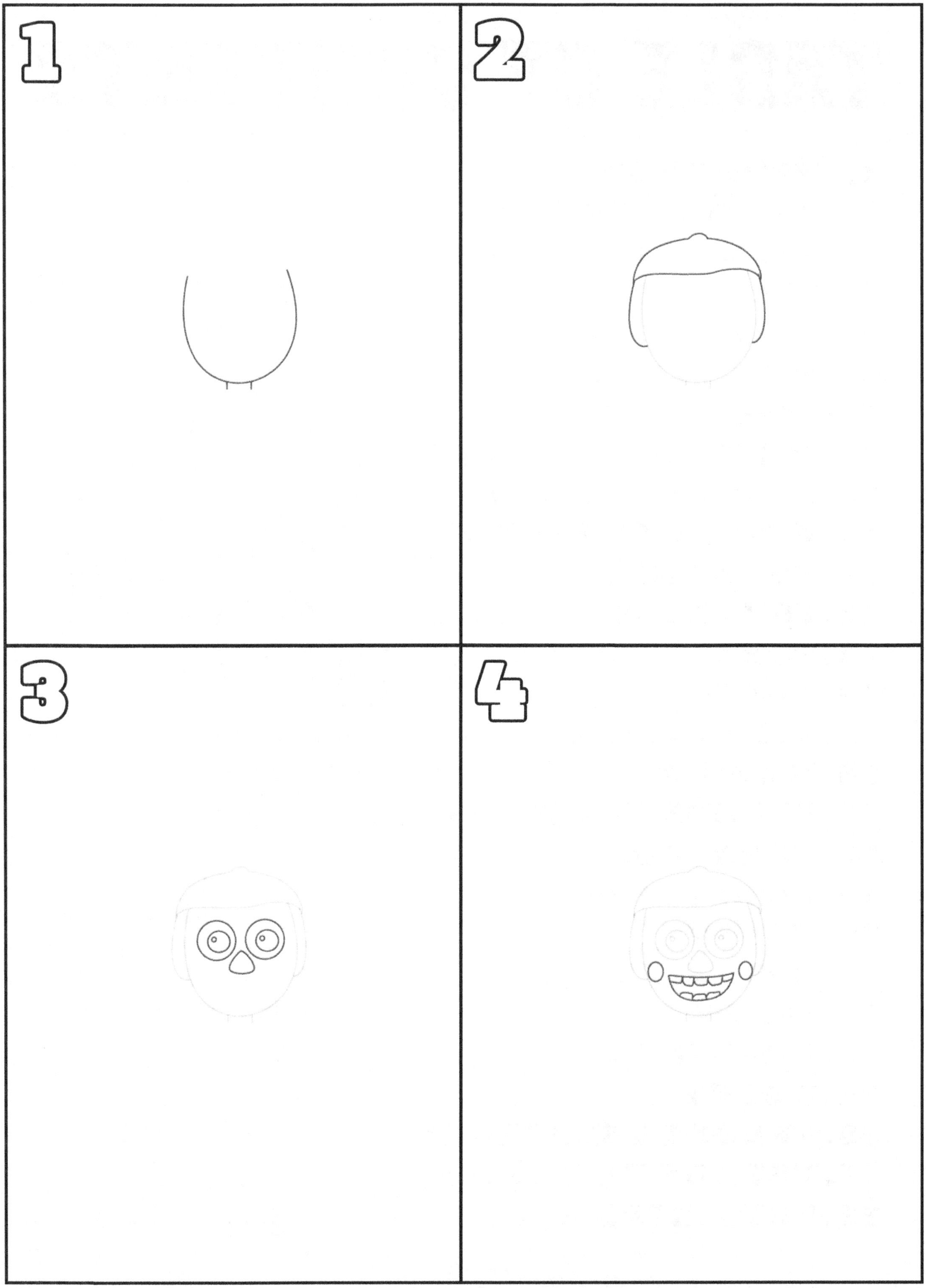
1
2
3
4

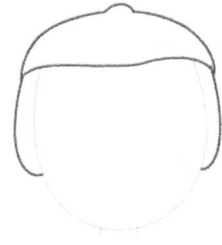

5

6

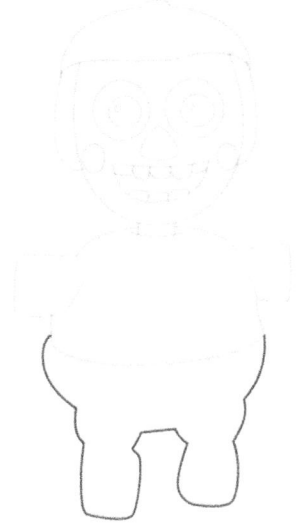

7

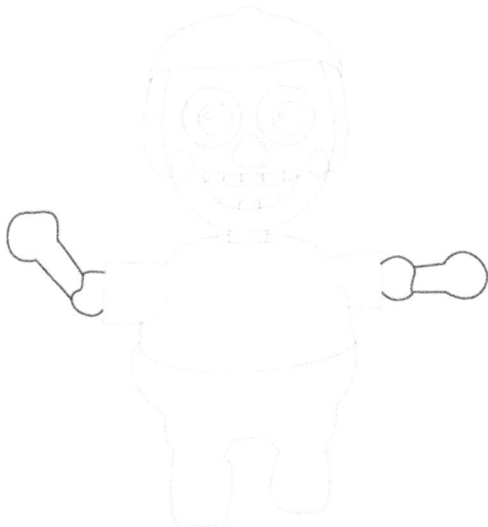

8

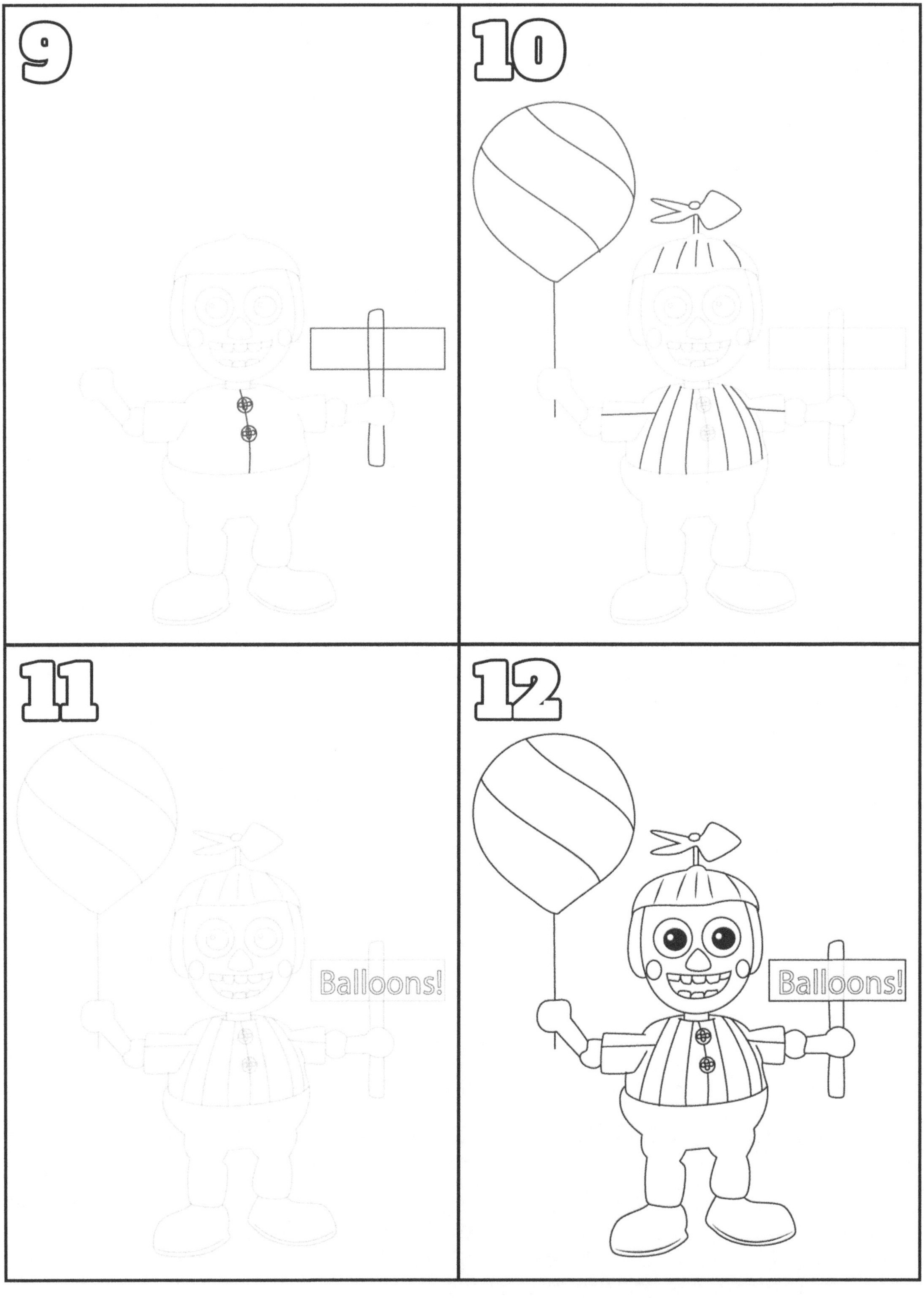
9
10
11
Balloons!
12
Balloons!

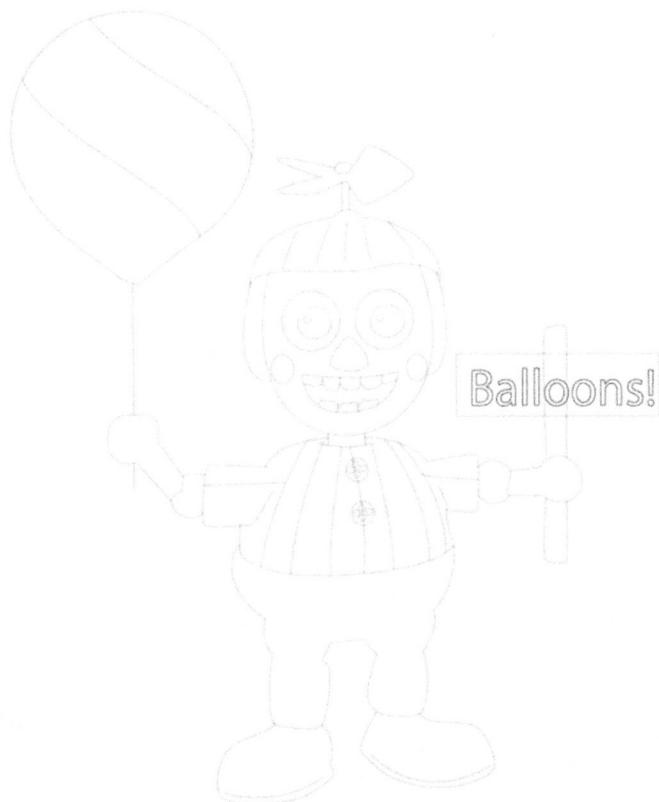

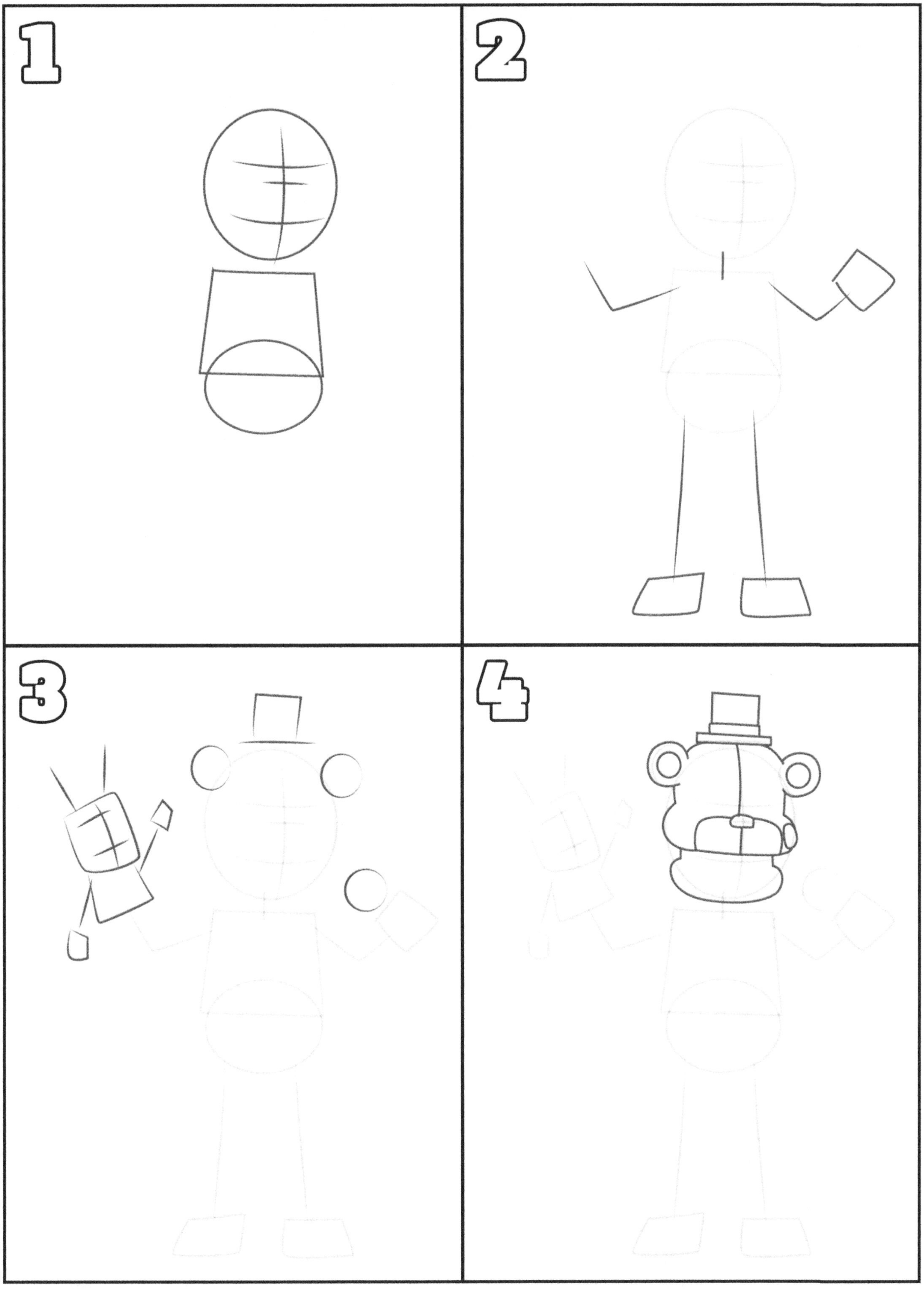
1
2
3
4

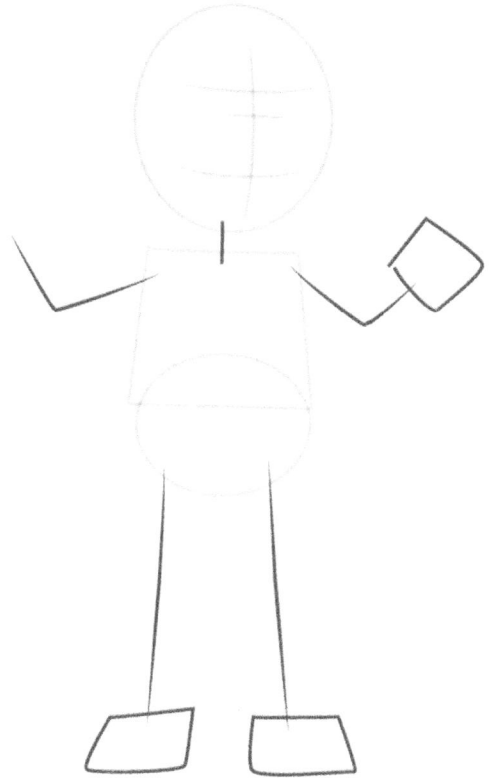

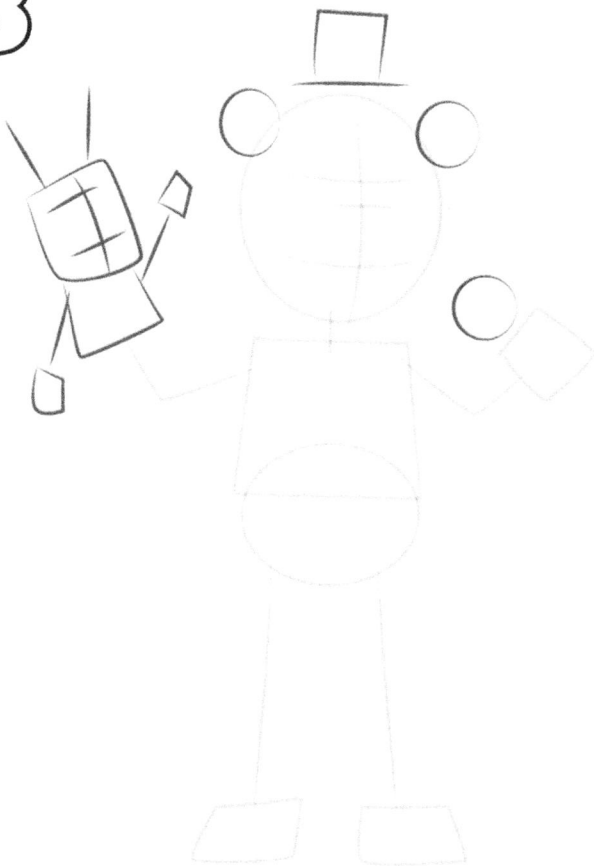

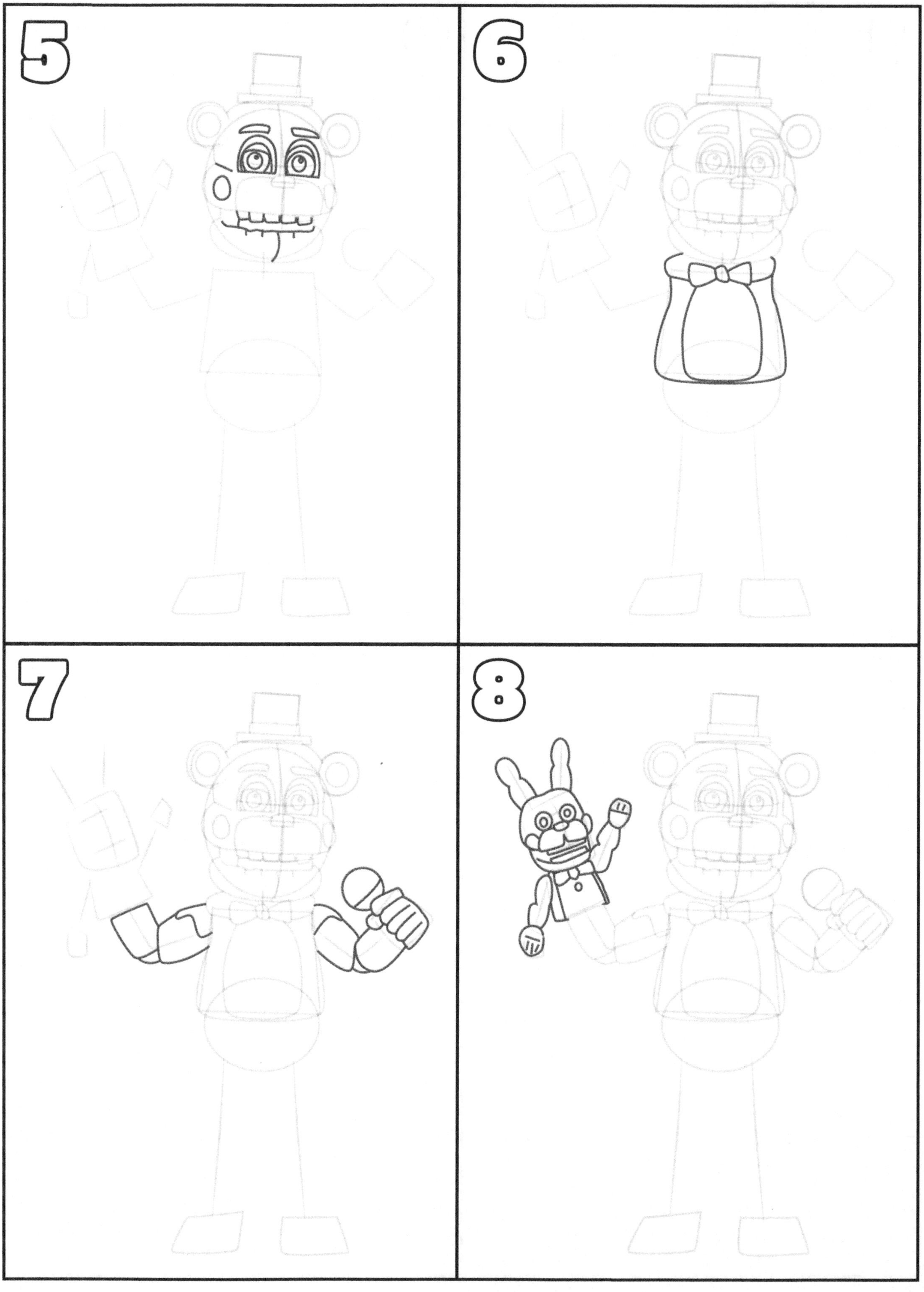
5
6
7
8

9

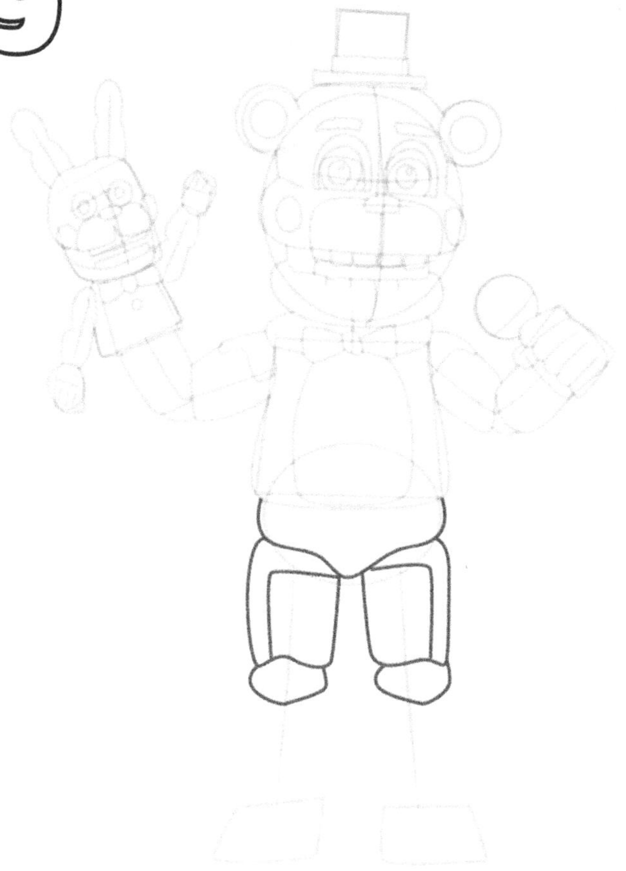

10

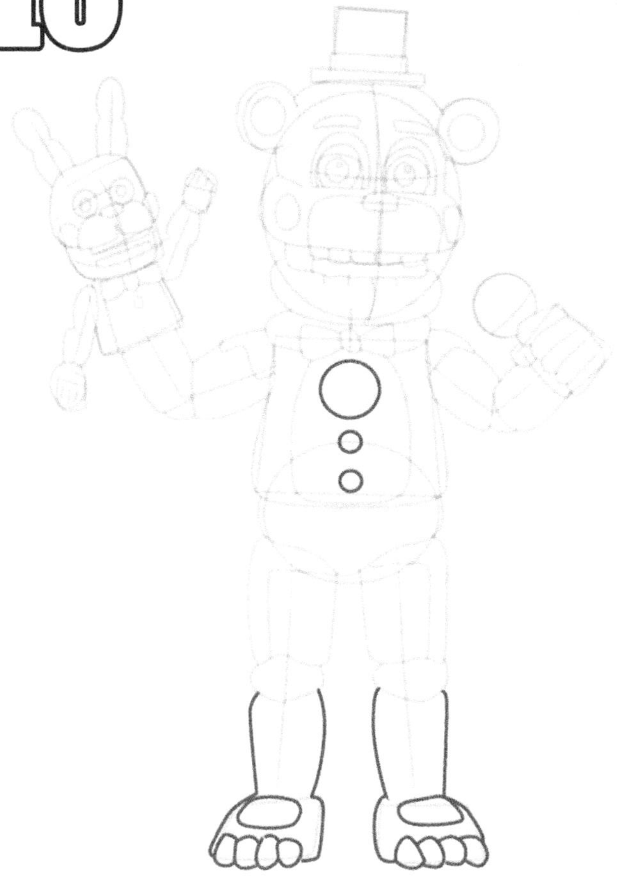

11

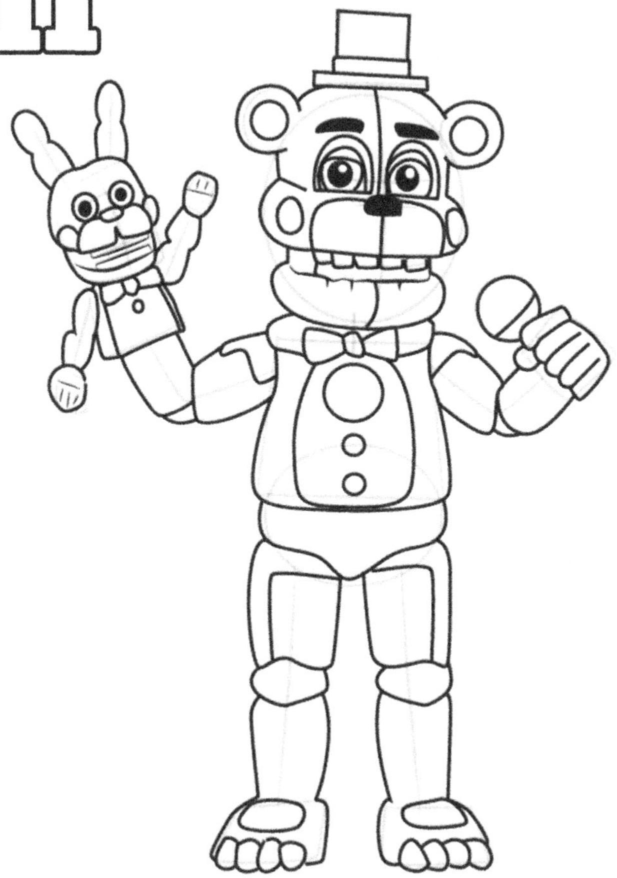

12

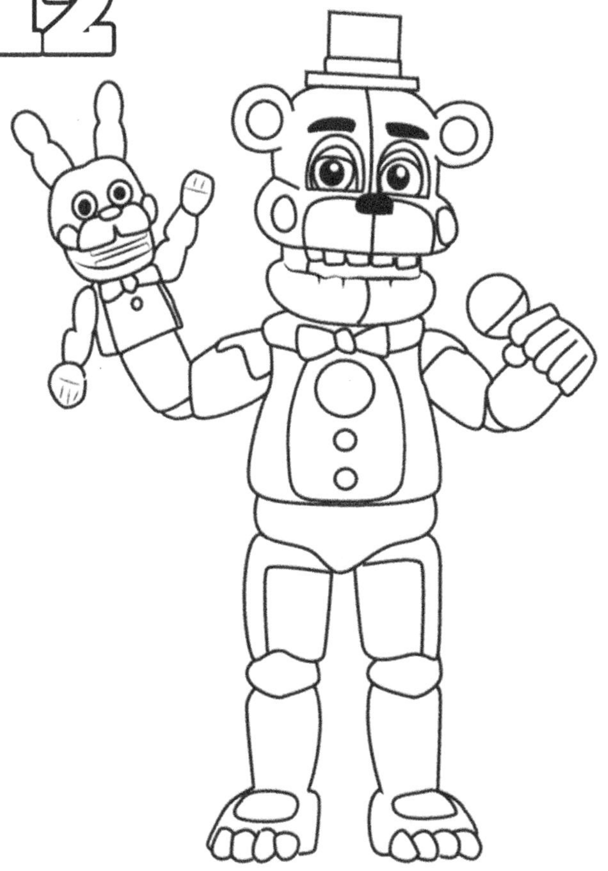

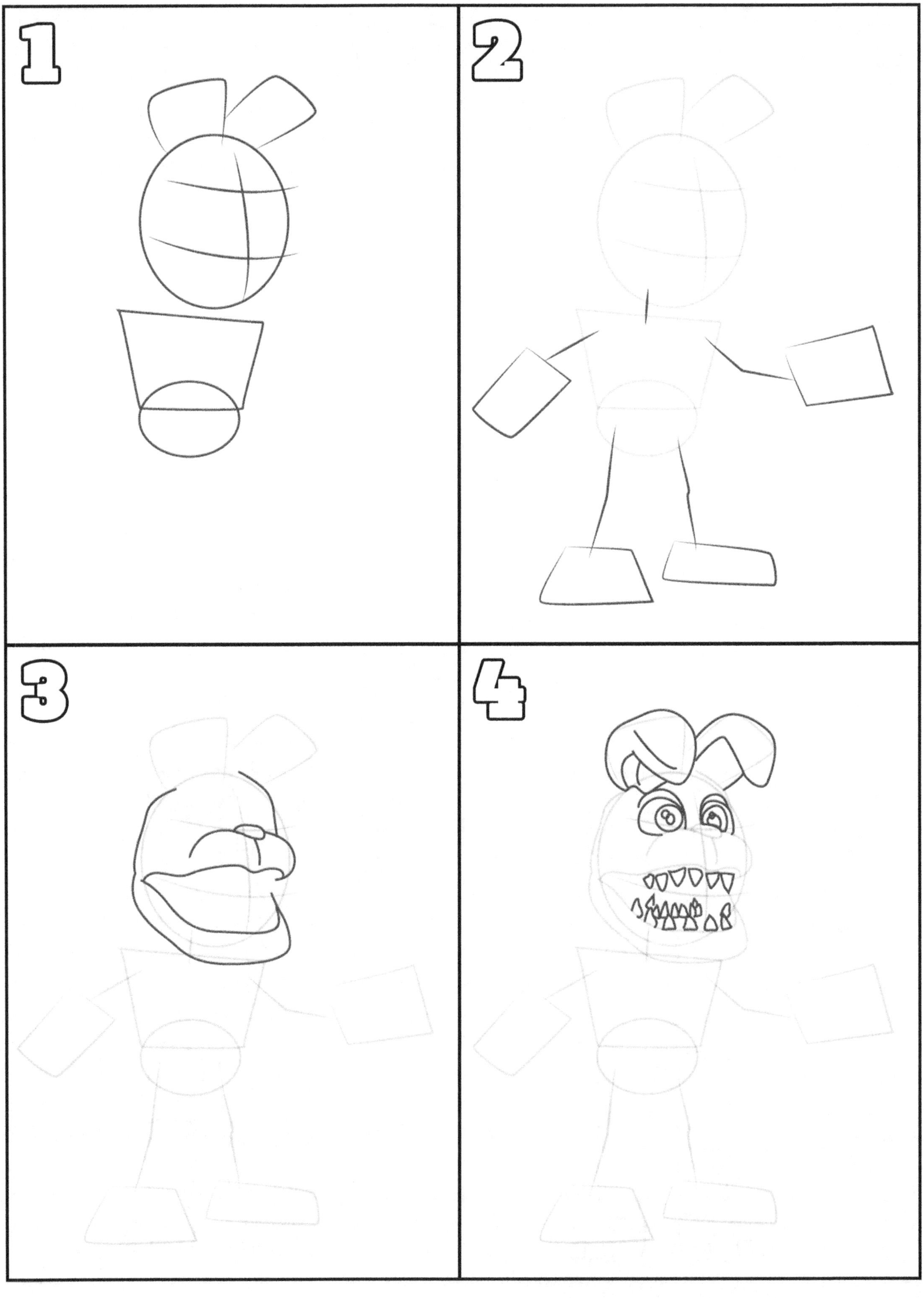
1
2
3
4

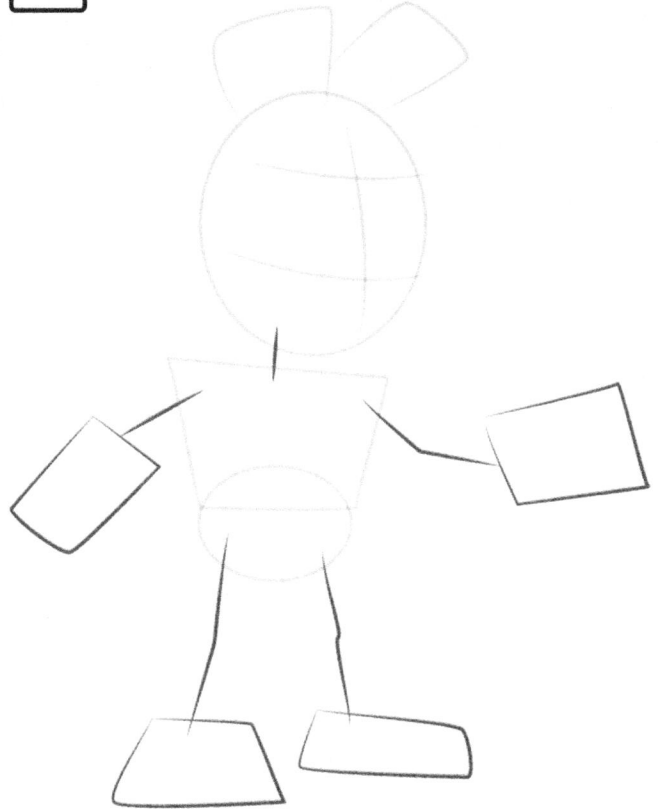

5

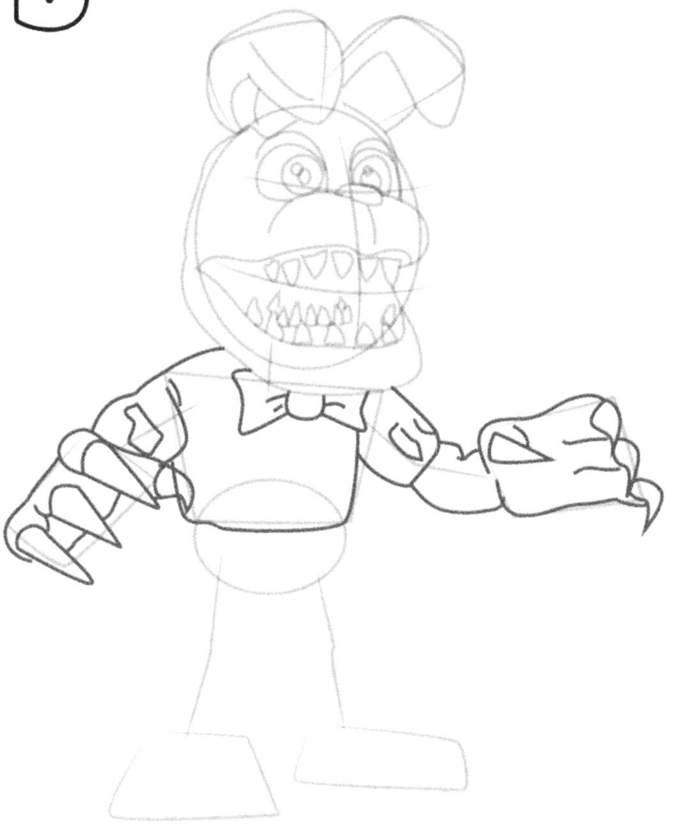

6

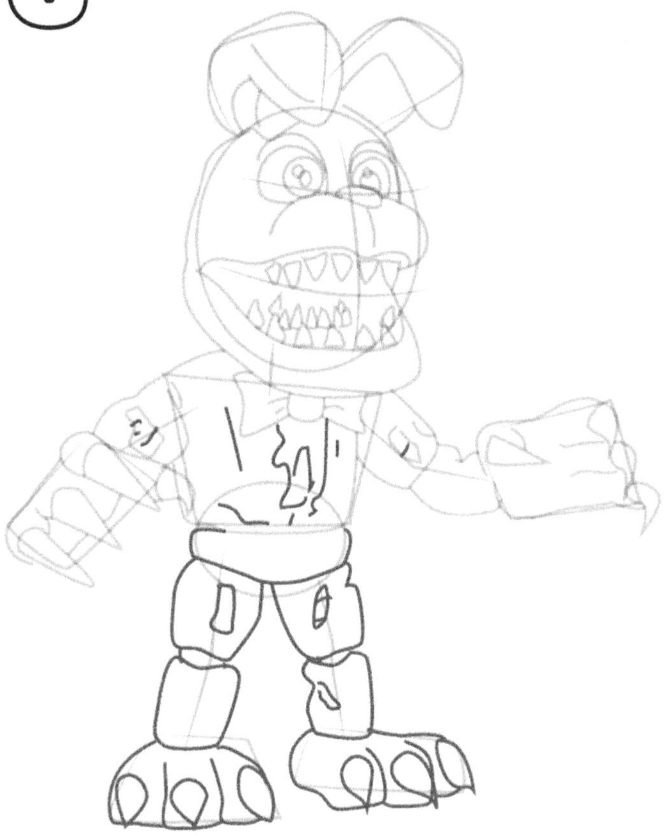

7

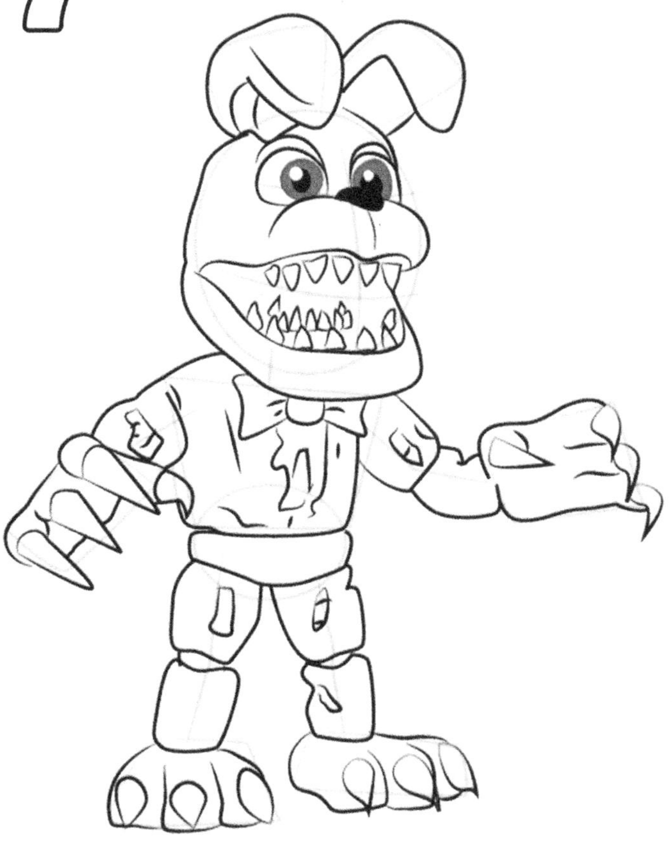

8

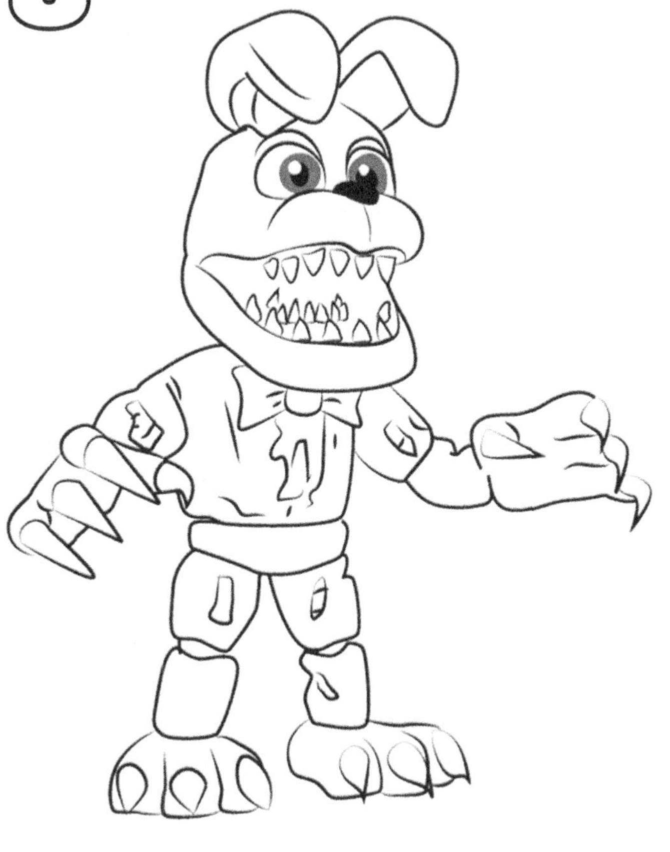

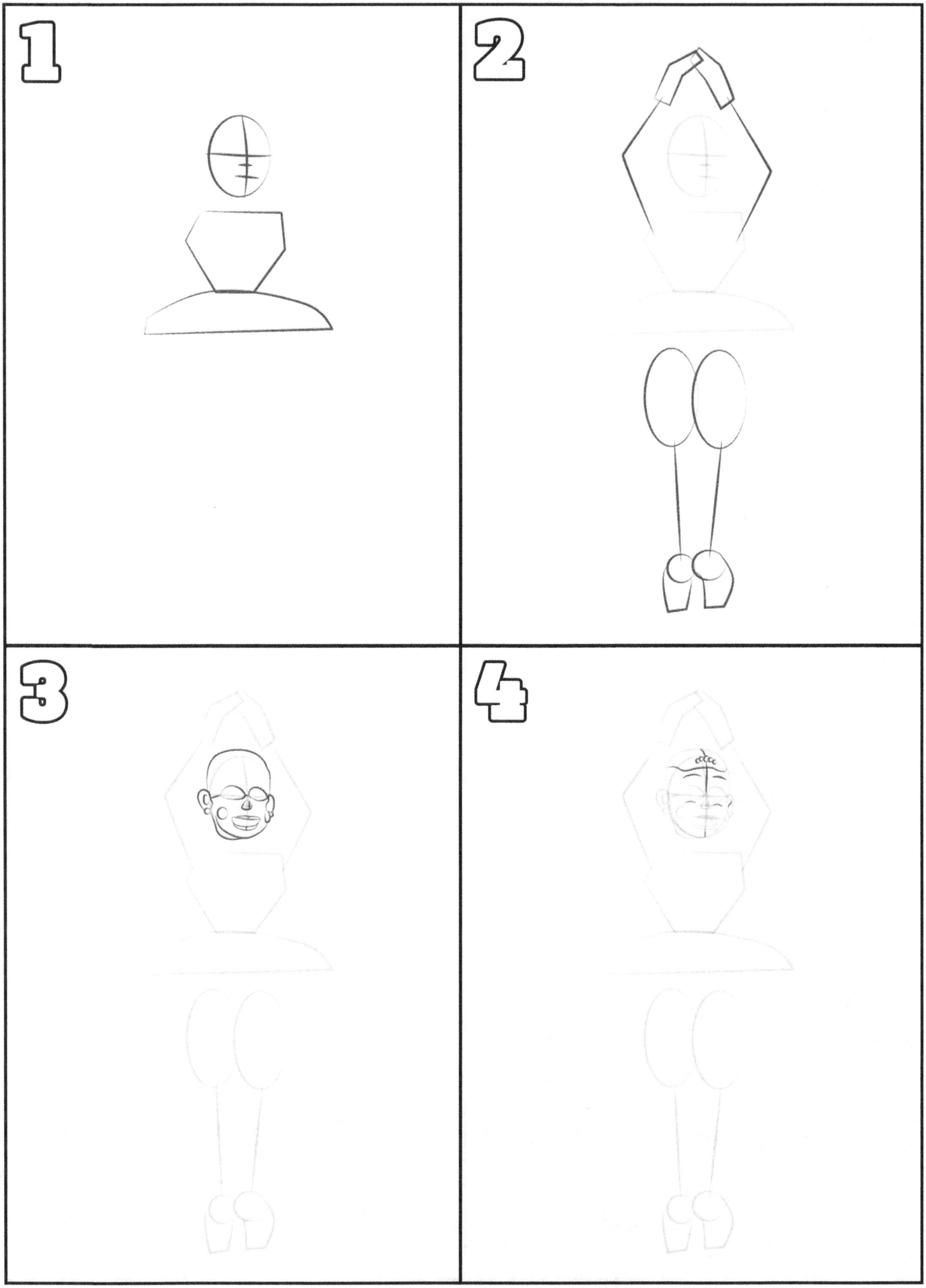
1
2
3
4

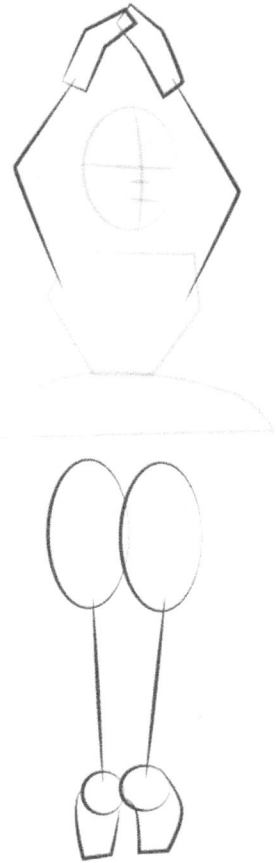

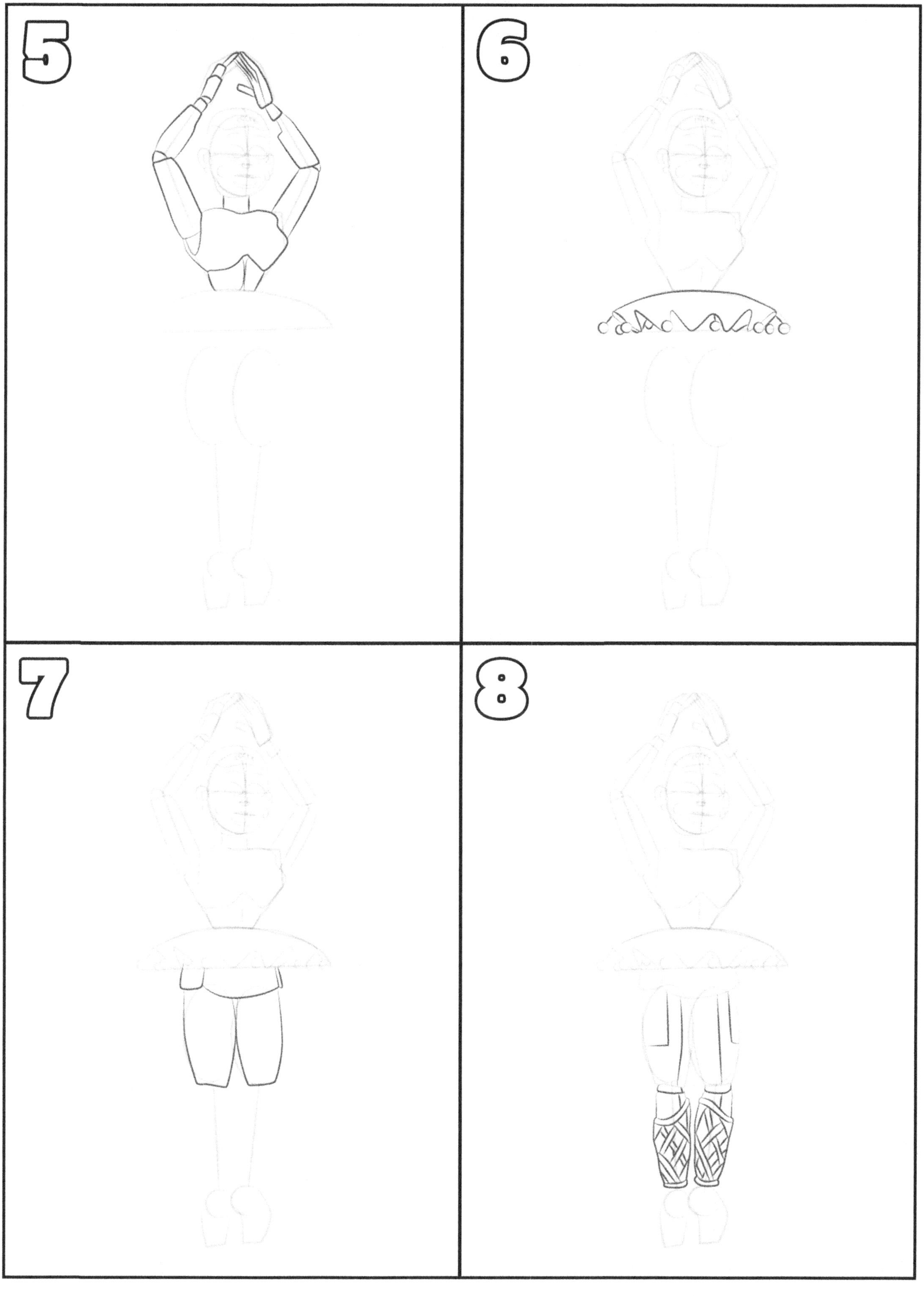
5
6
7
8

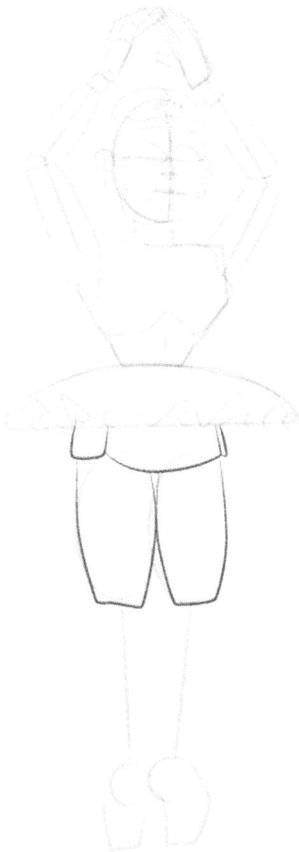

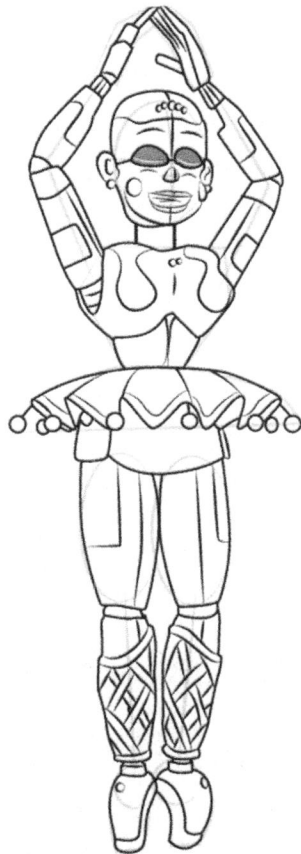

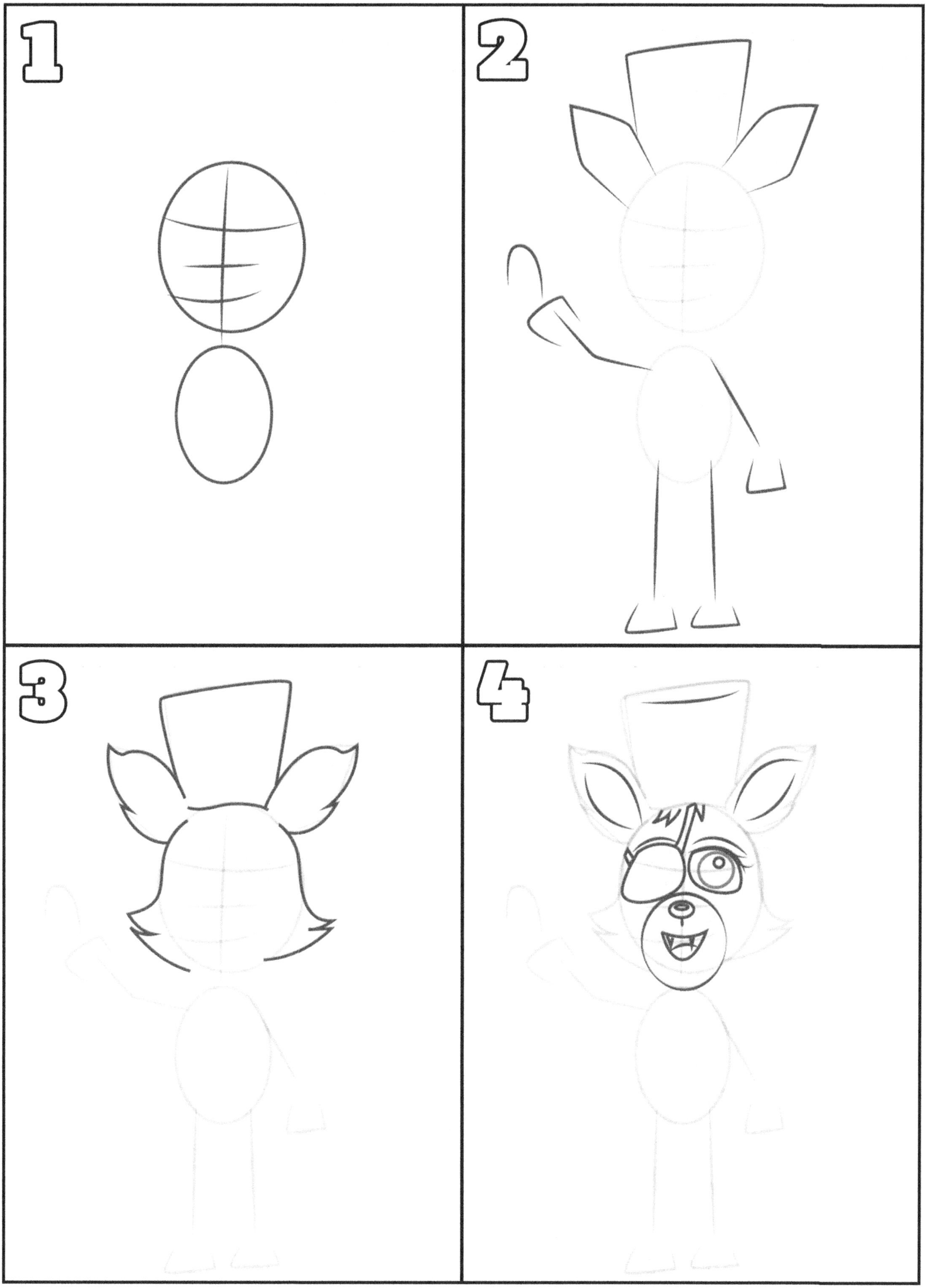
1
2
3
4

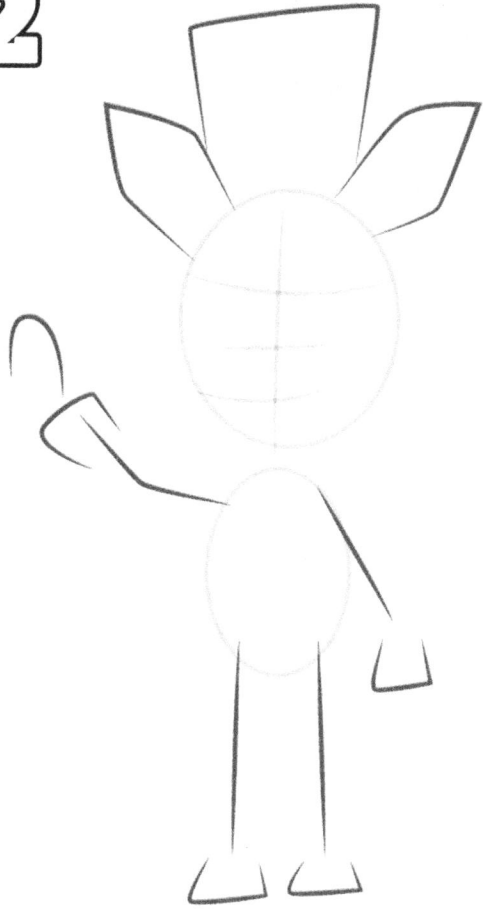

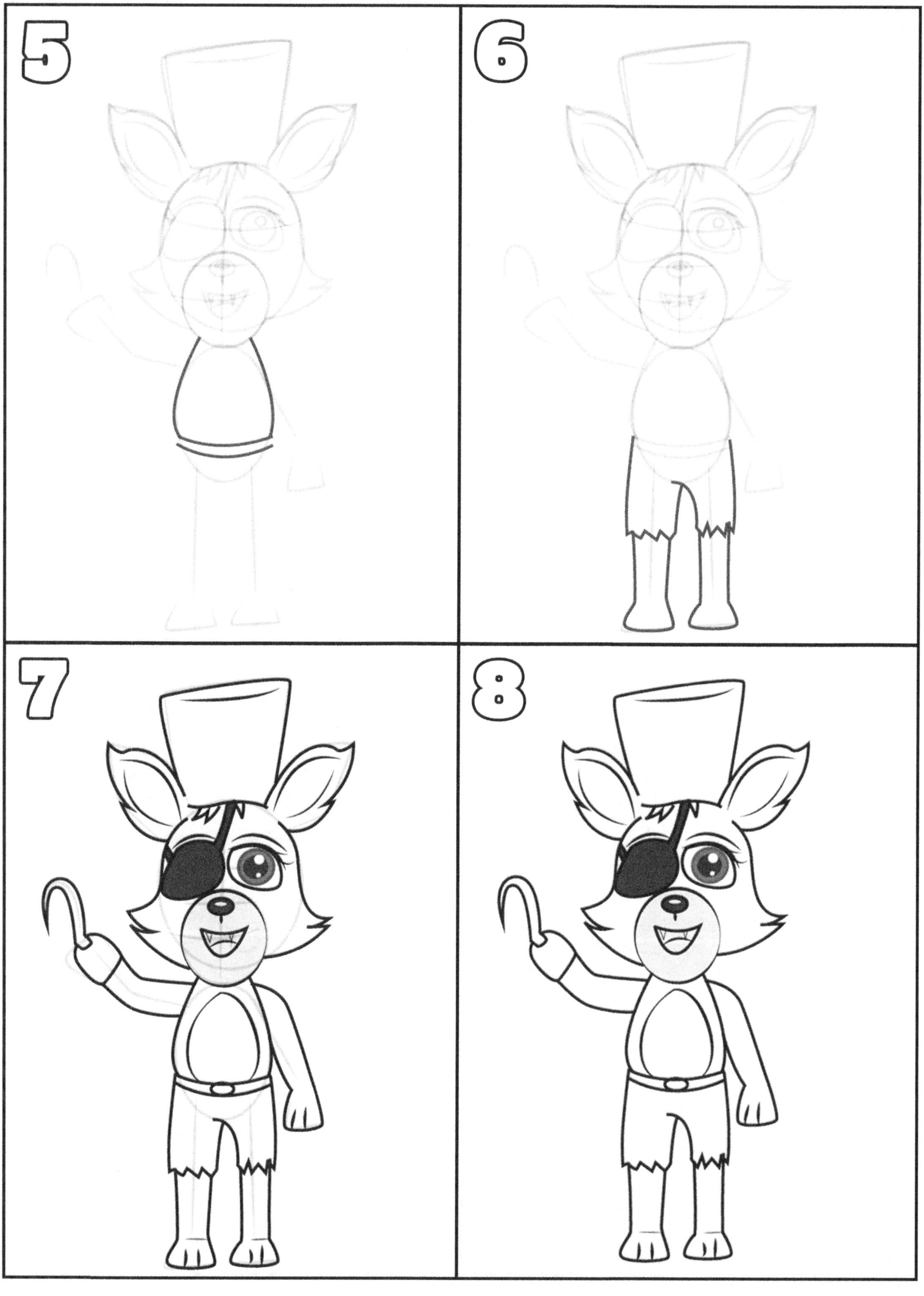
5
6
7
8

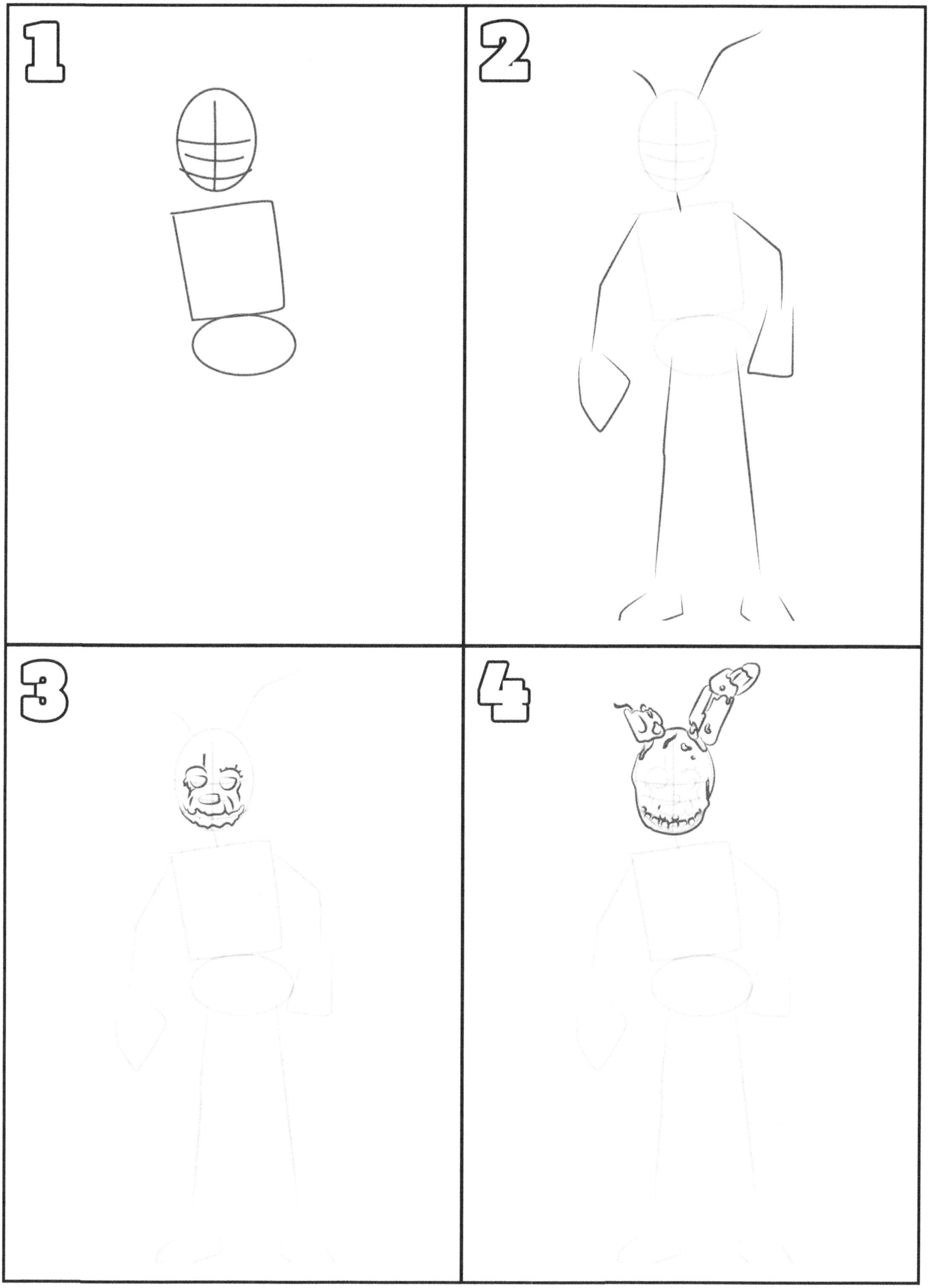
1
2
3
4

5

6

7

8

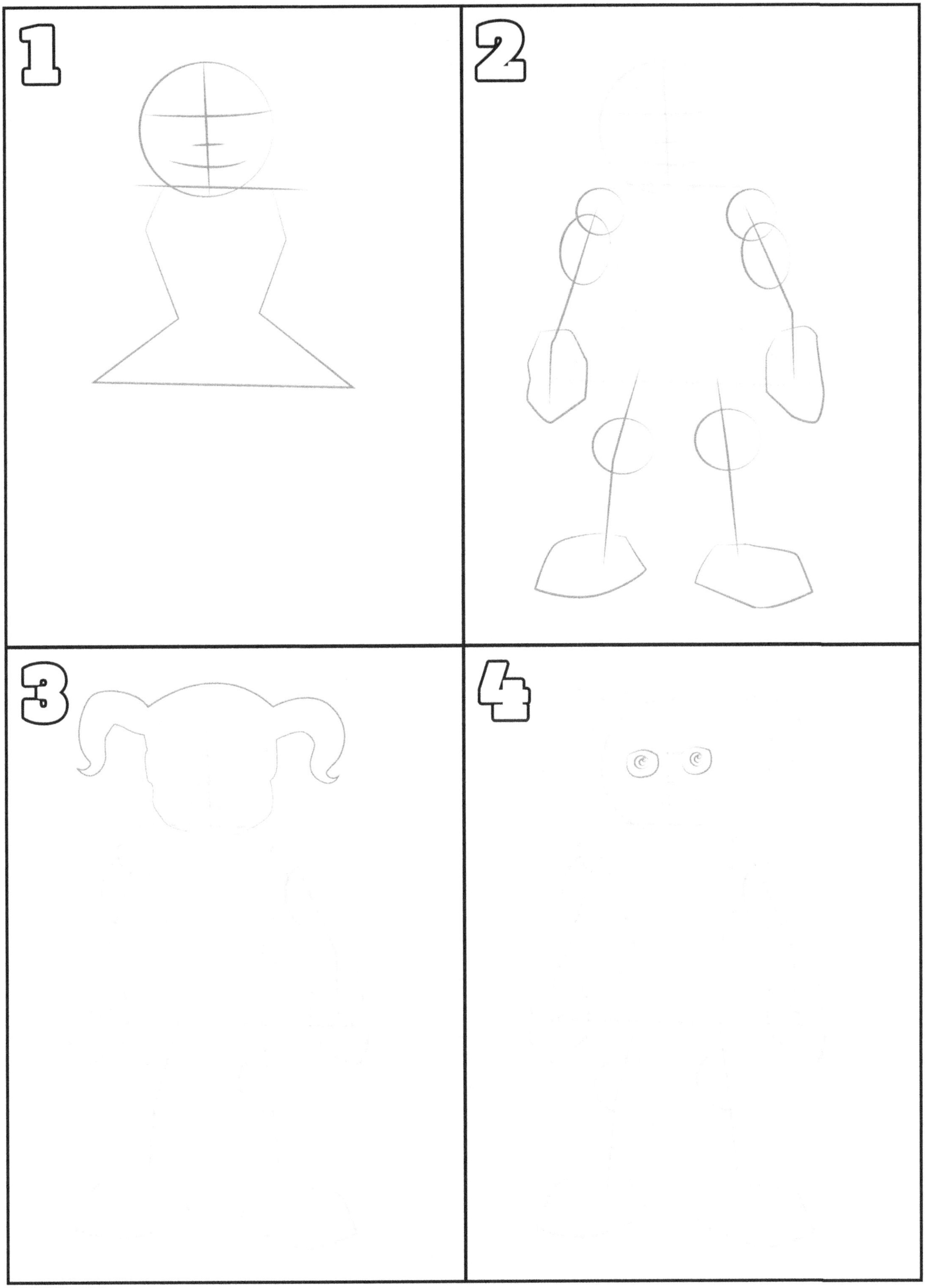
1
2
3
4

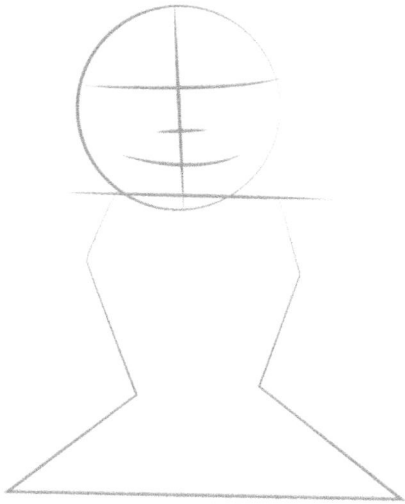

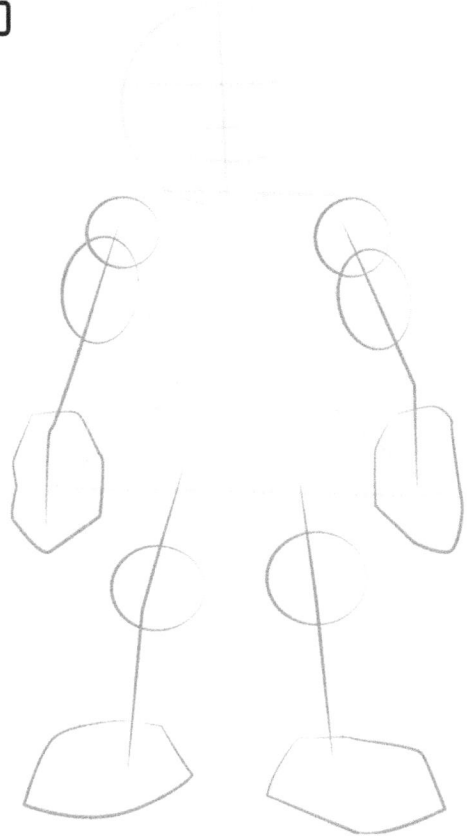

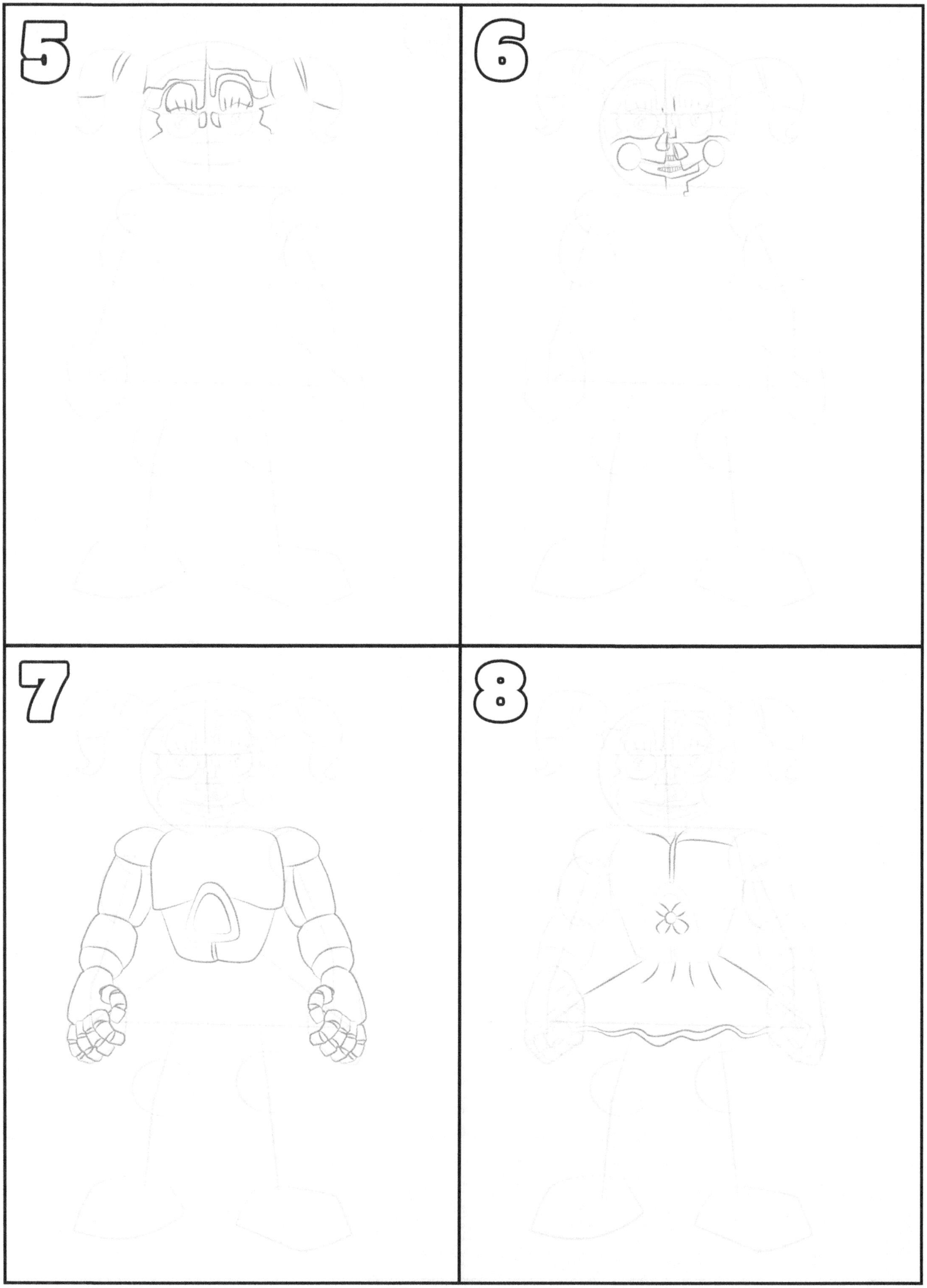
5
6
7
8

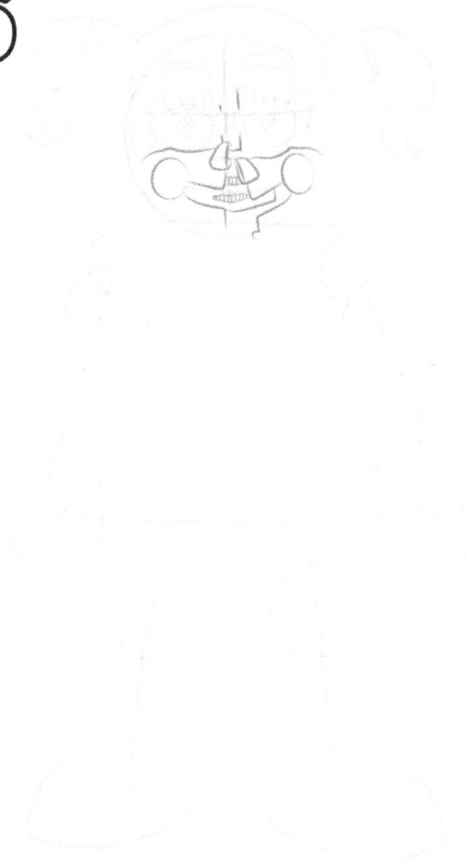

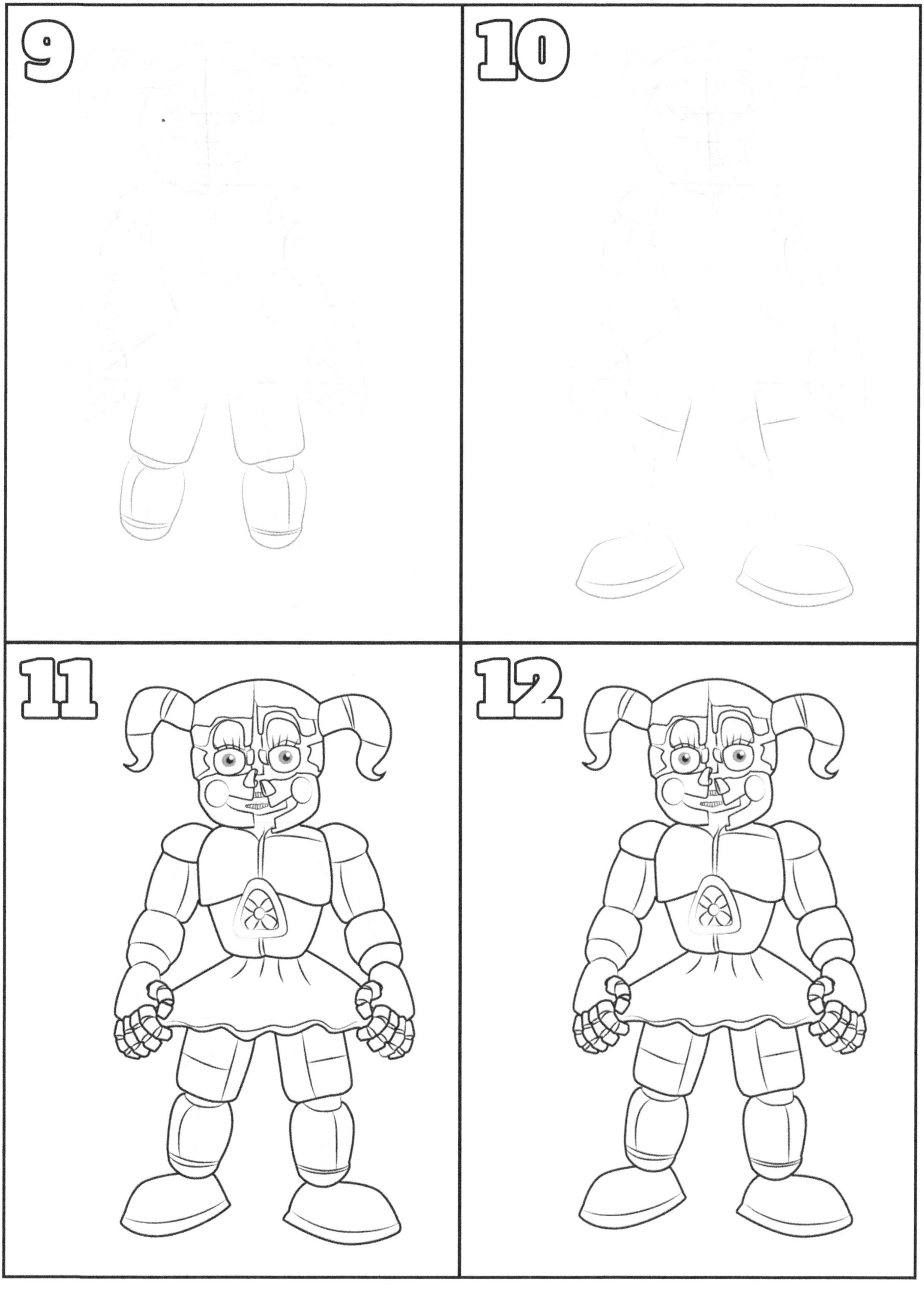
9
10
11
12

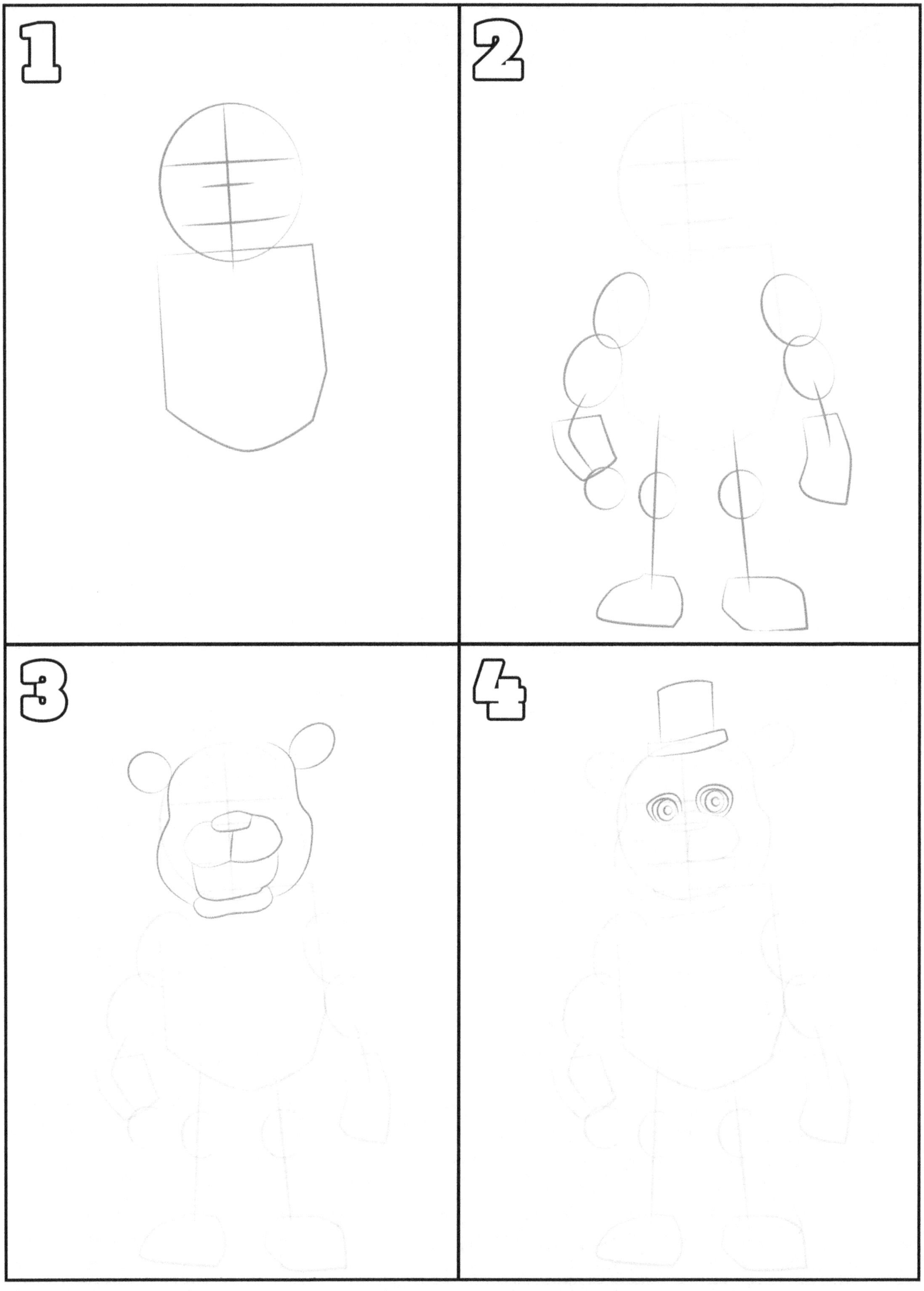
1
2
3
4

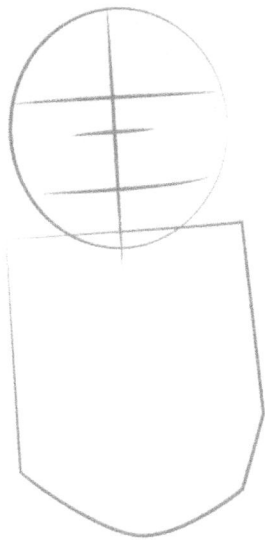

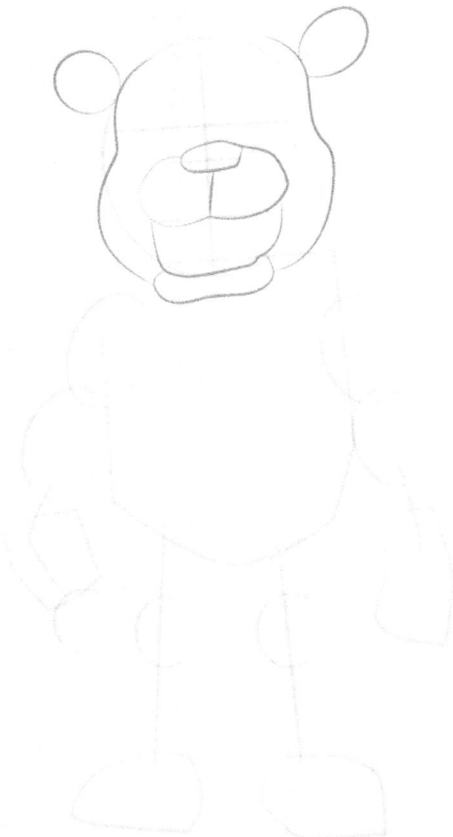

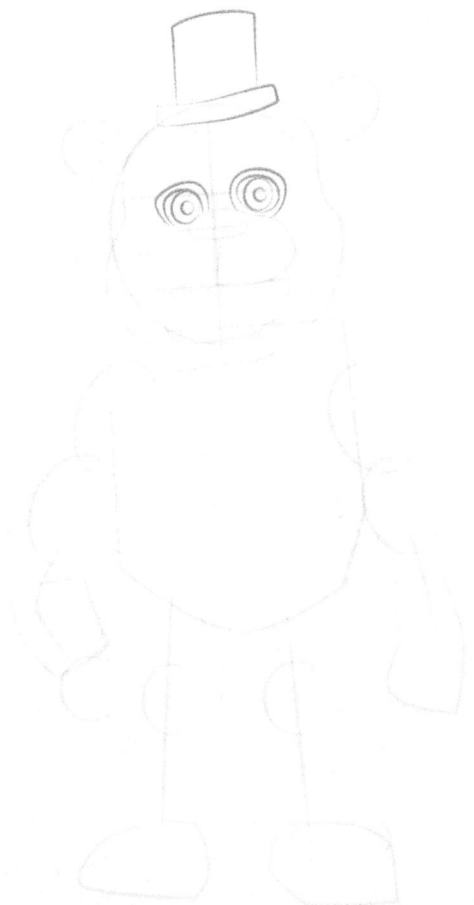

5

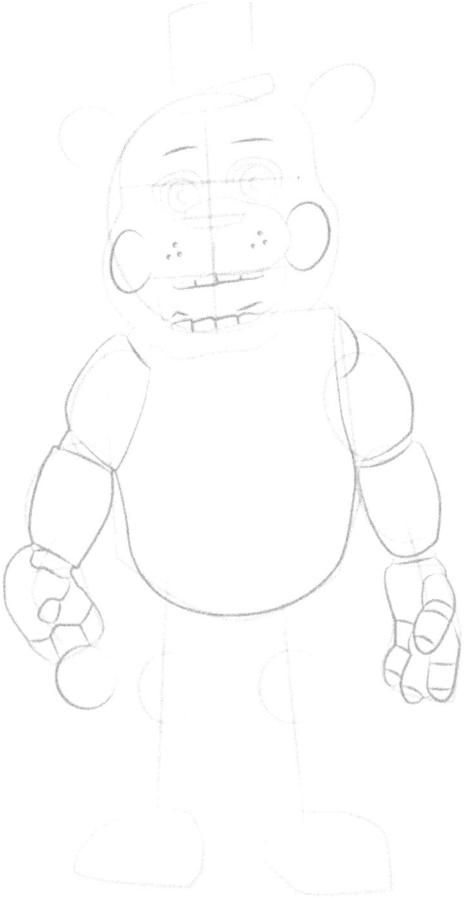

6

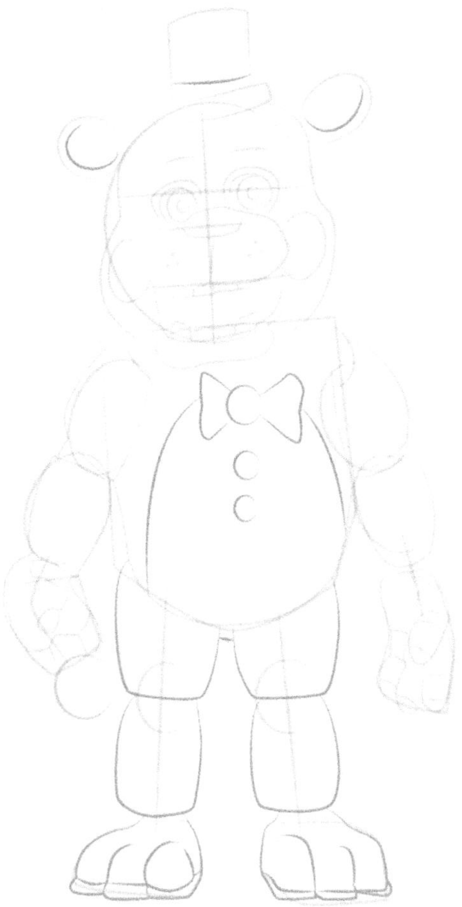

7

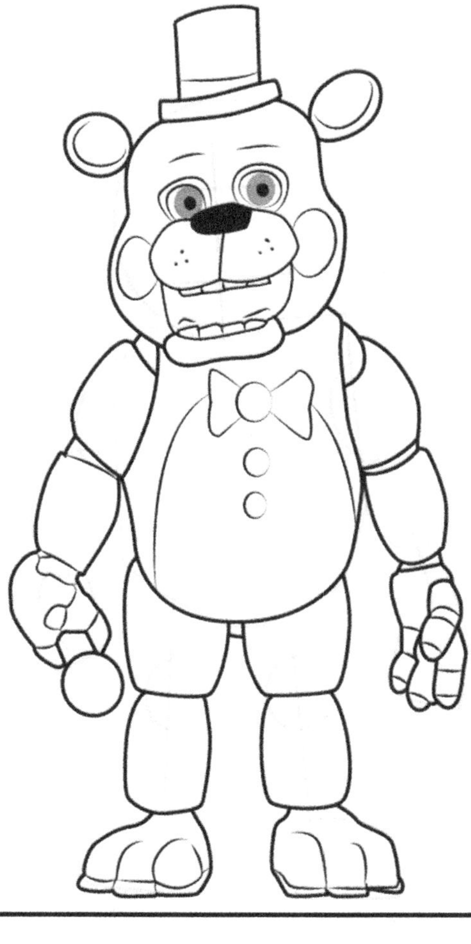

8

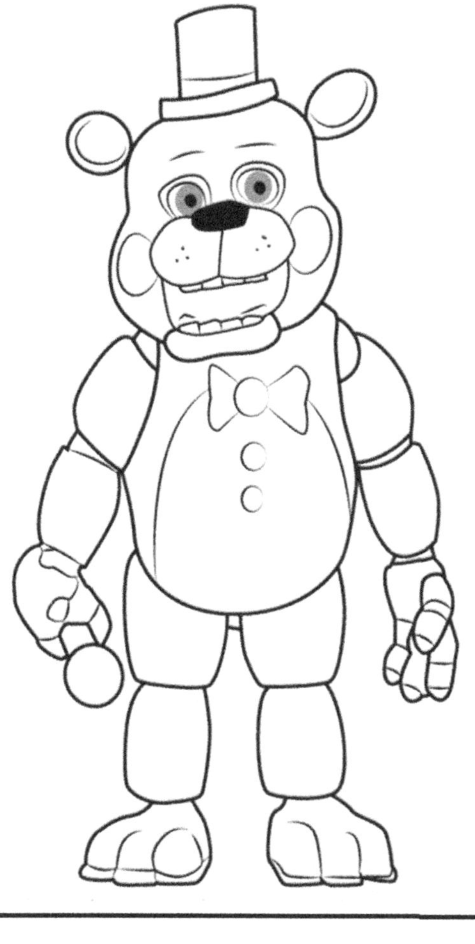

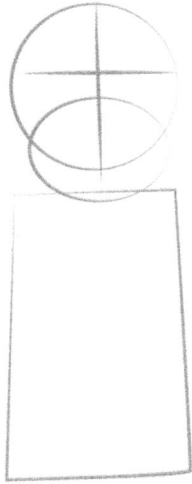

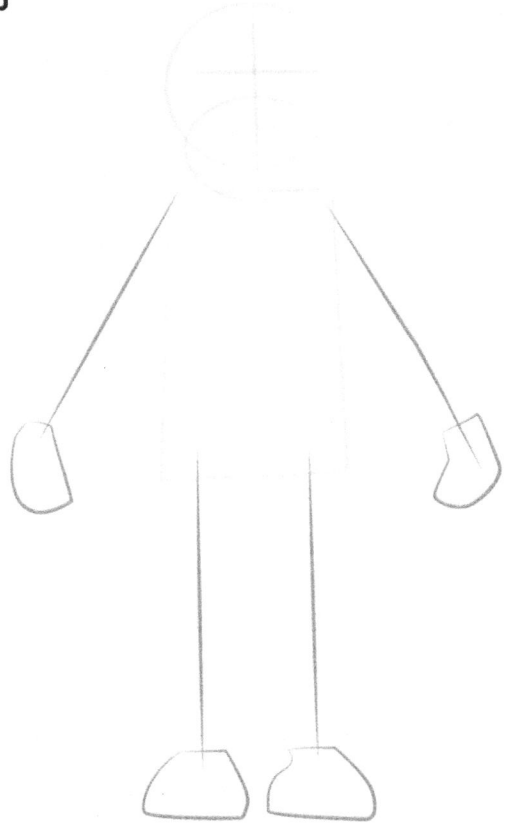

5

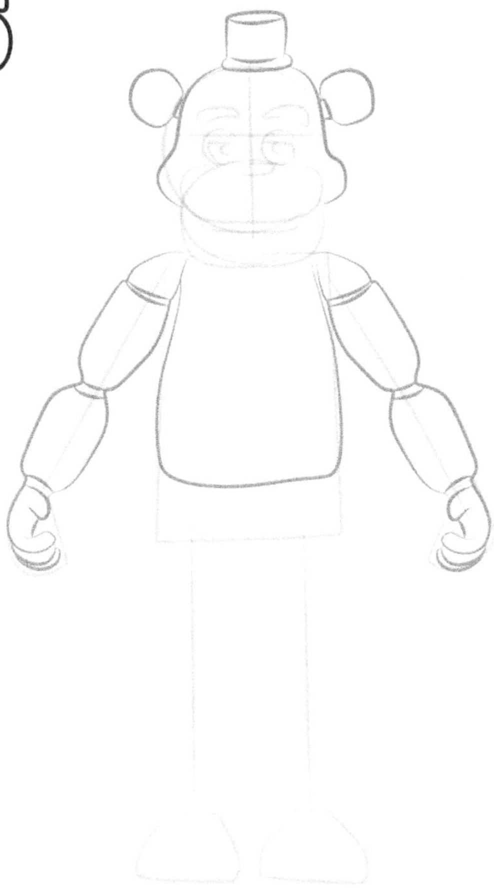

6

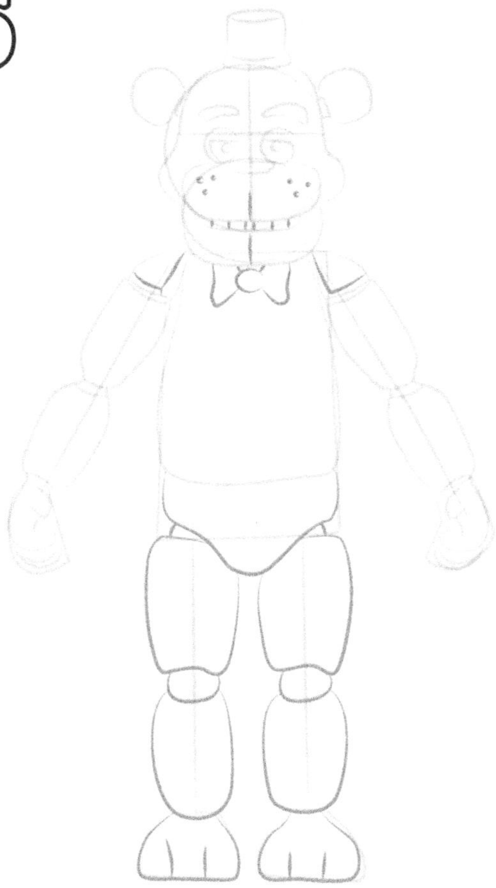

7

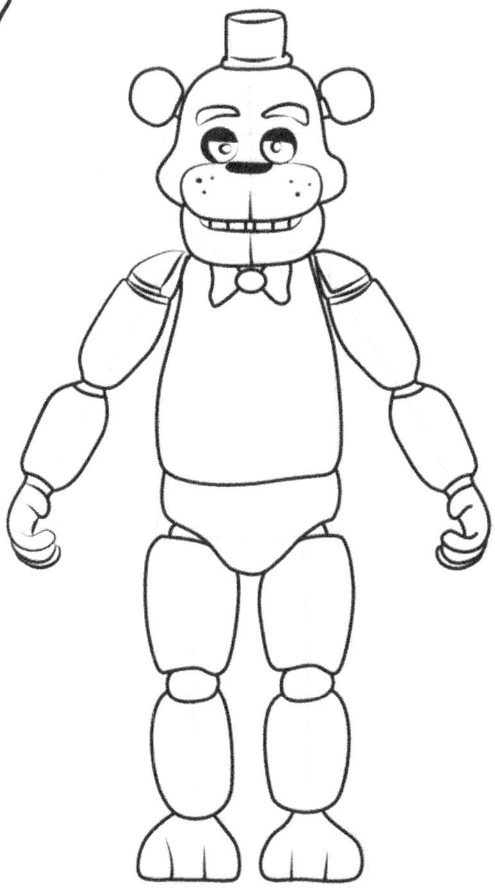

8

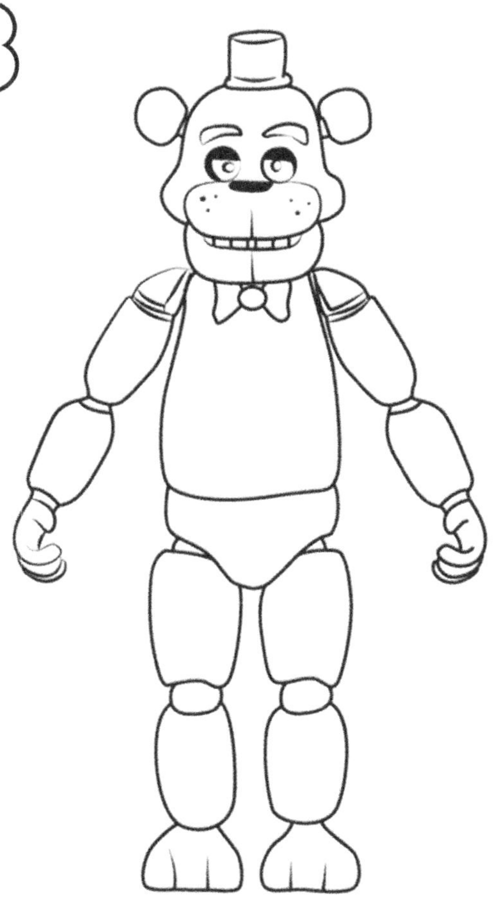

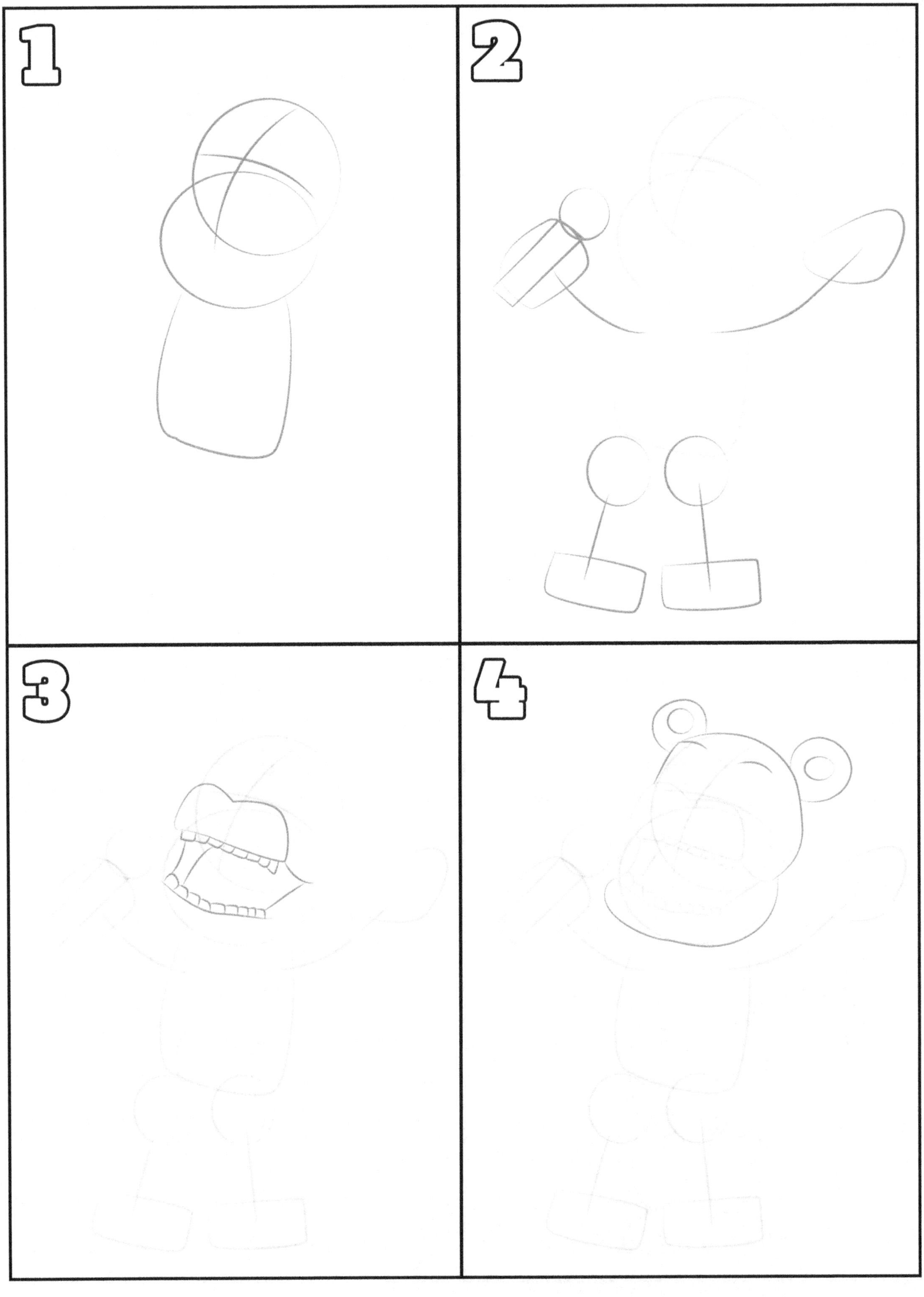
1
2
3
4

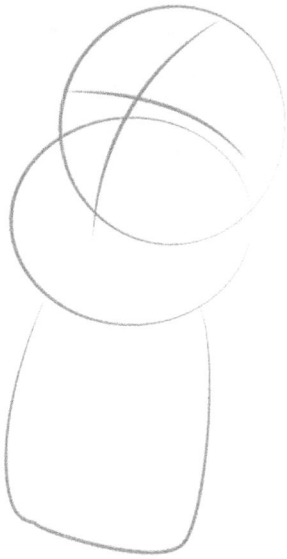

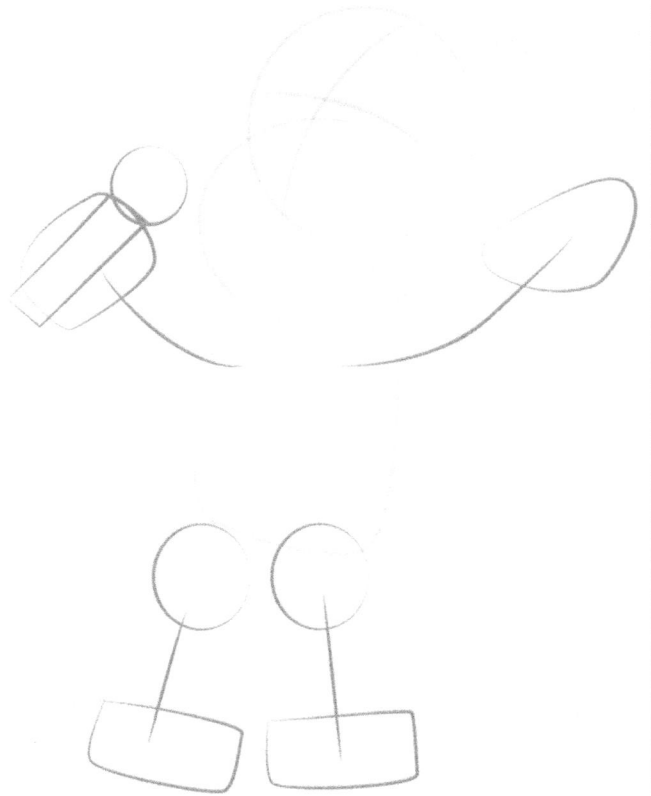

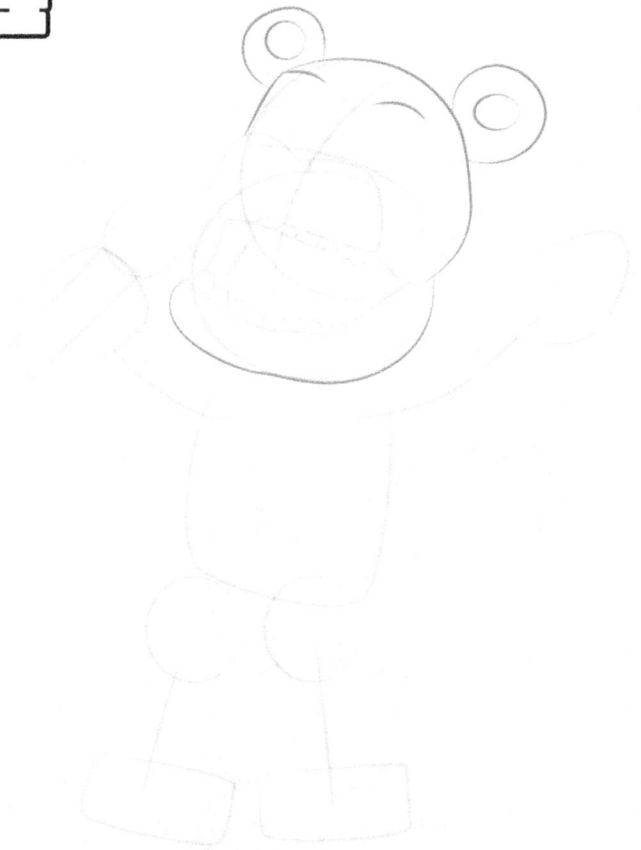

5

6

7

8

9

10

11

12

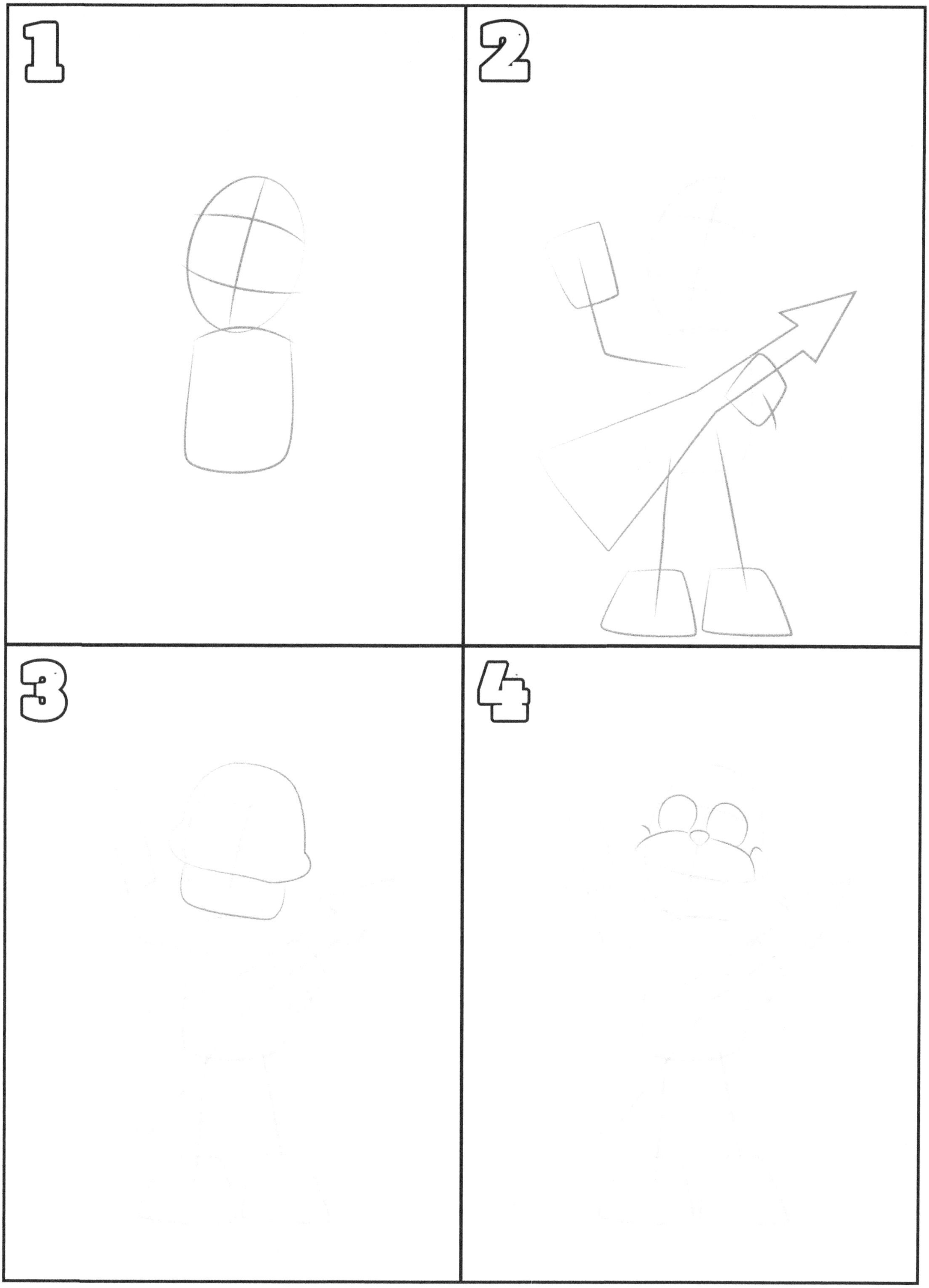
1
2
3
4

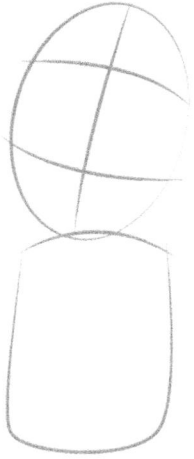

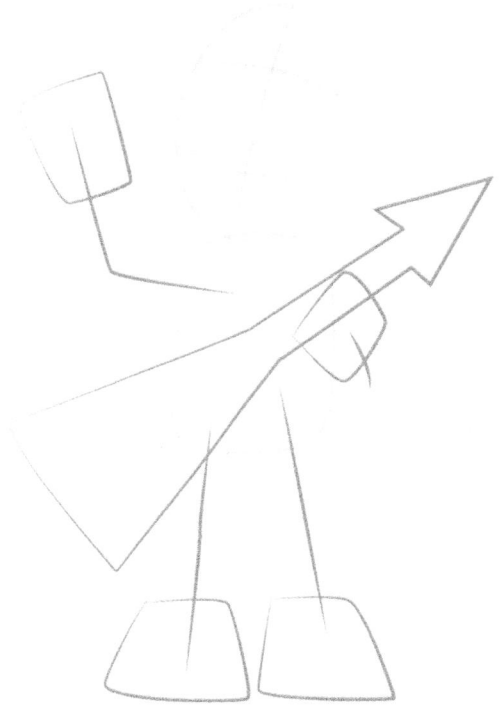

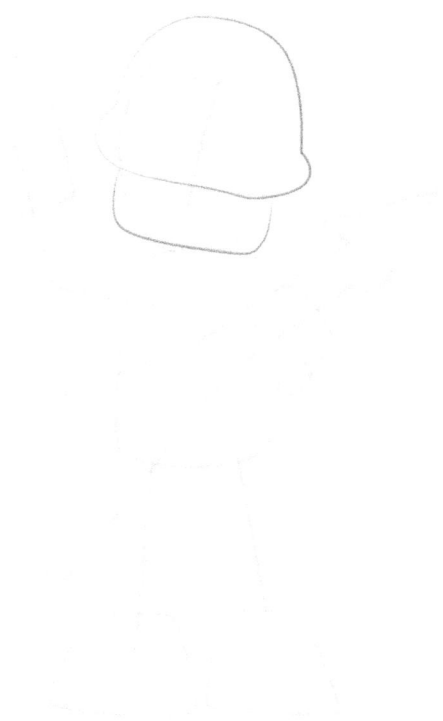

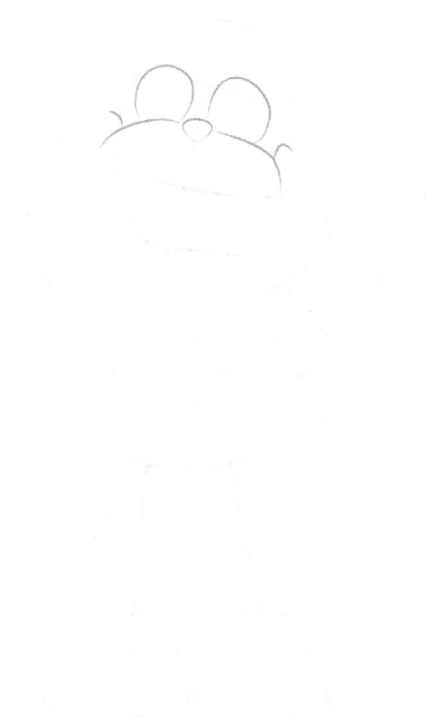

5

6

7

8

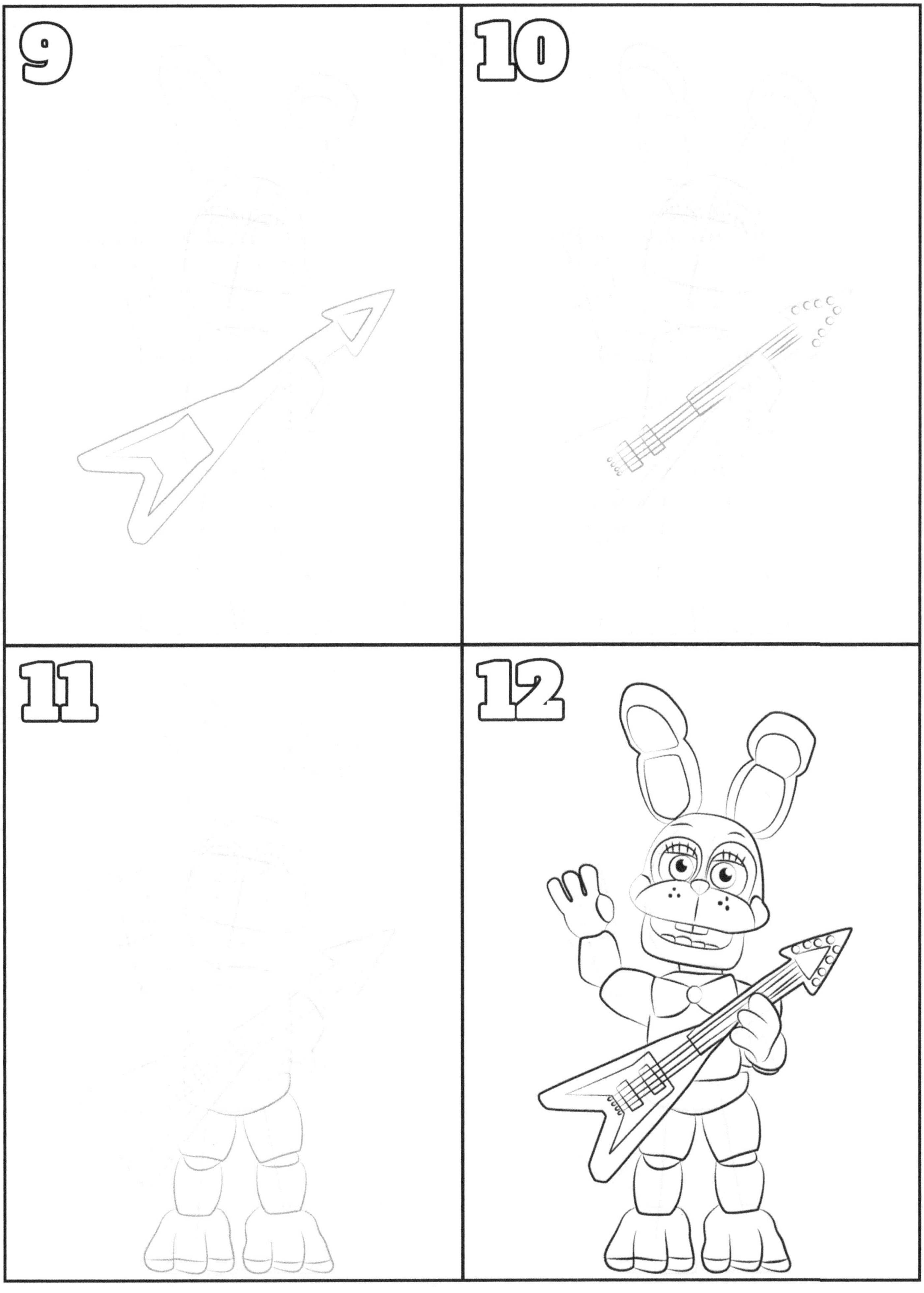
9
10
11
12

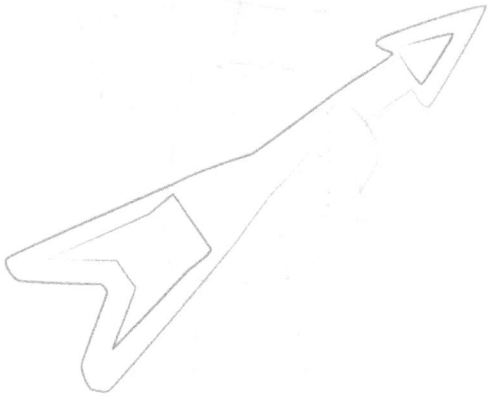

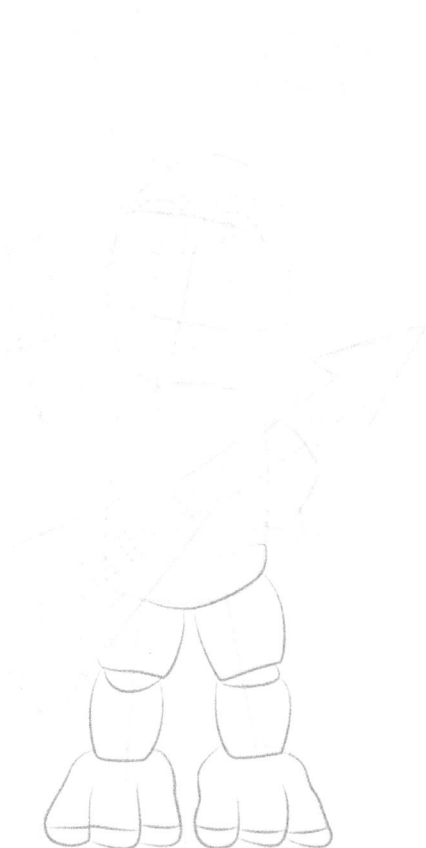

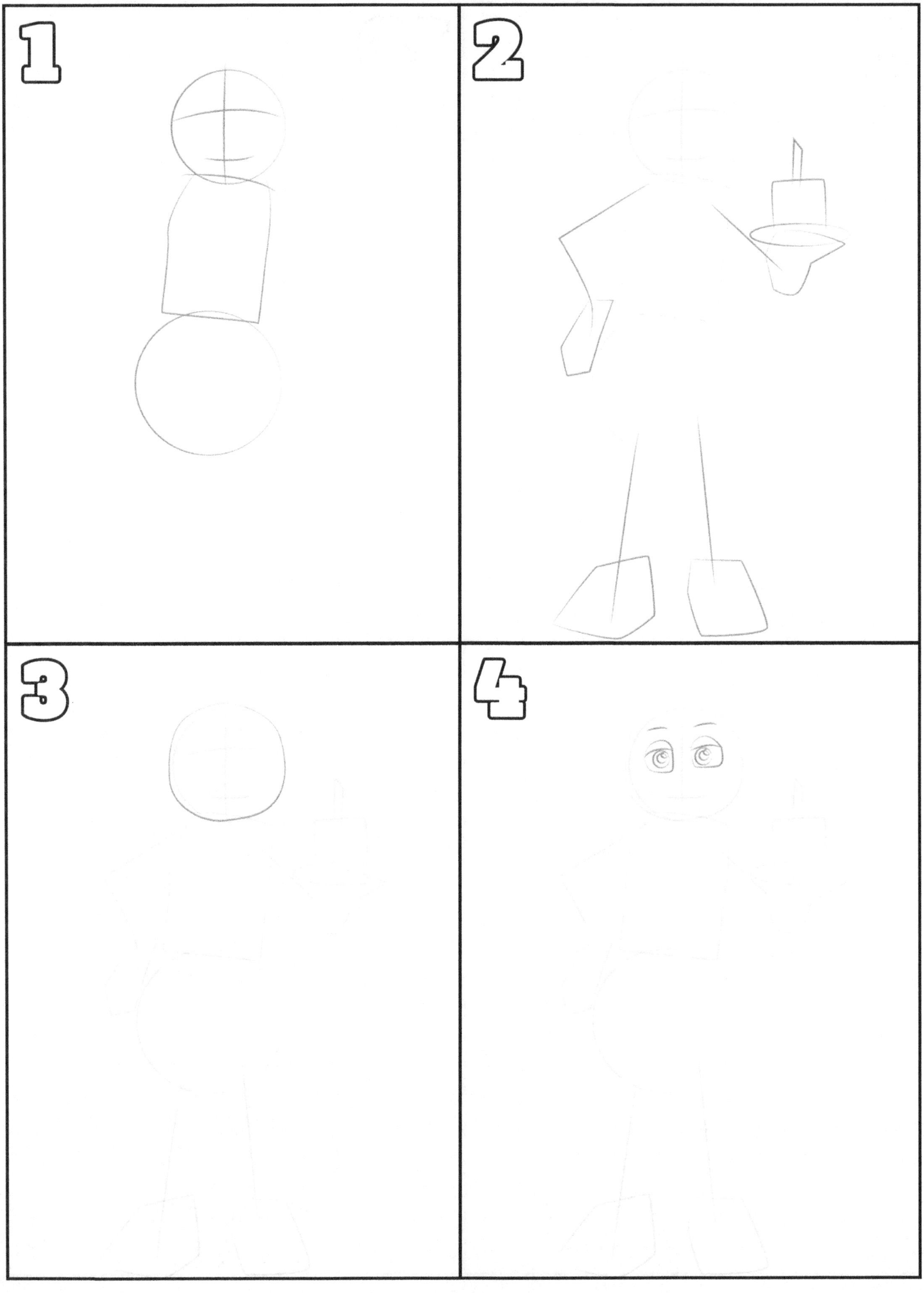
1
2
3
4

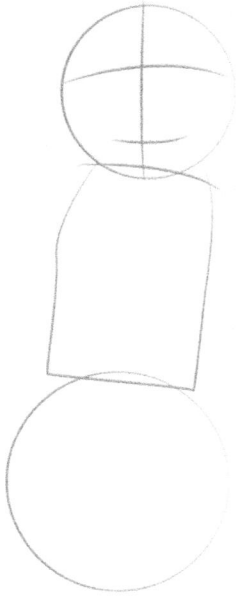

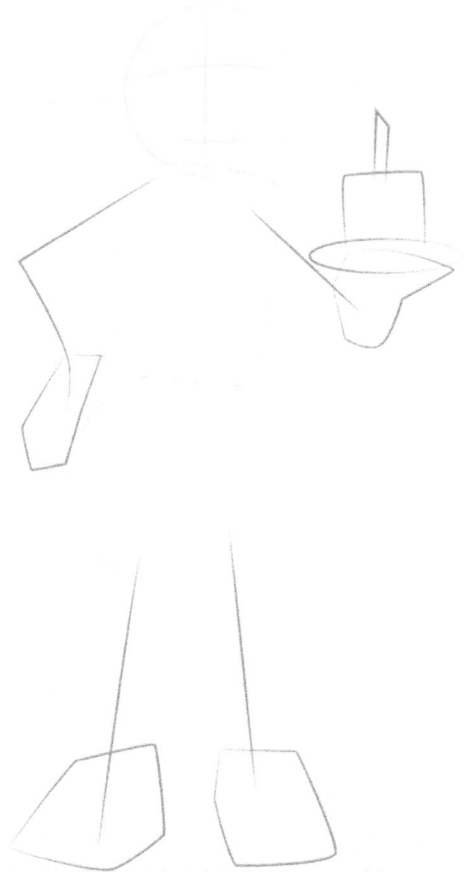

5

6

7

8

9

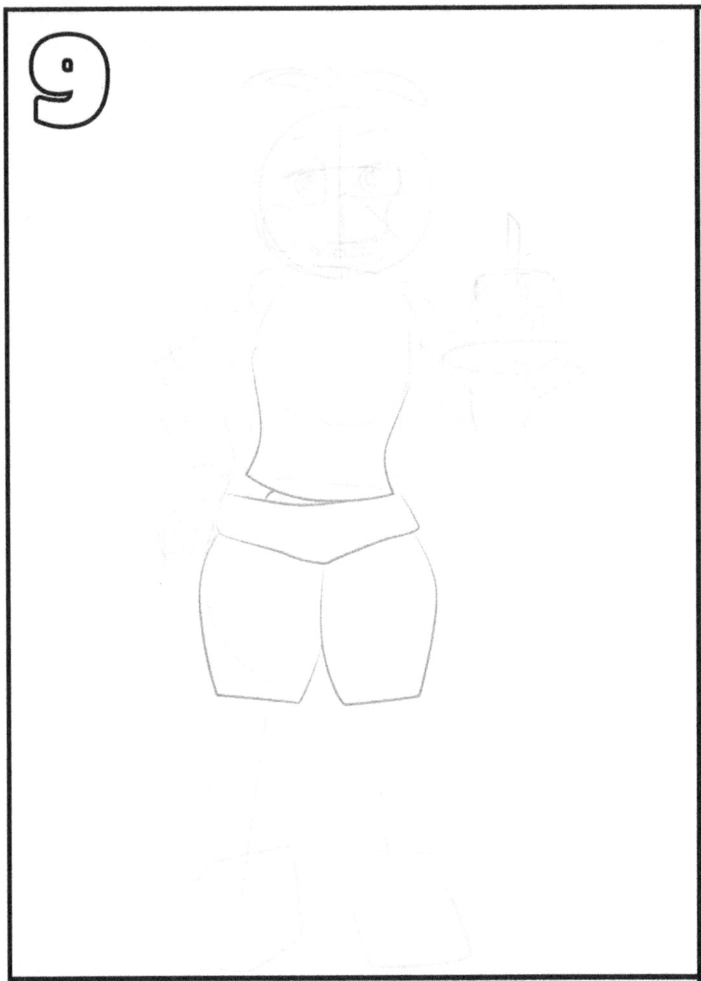

10

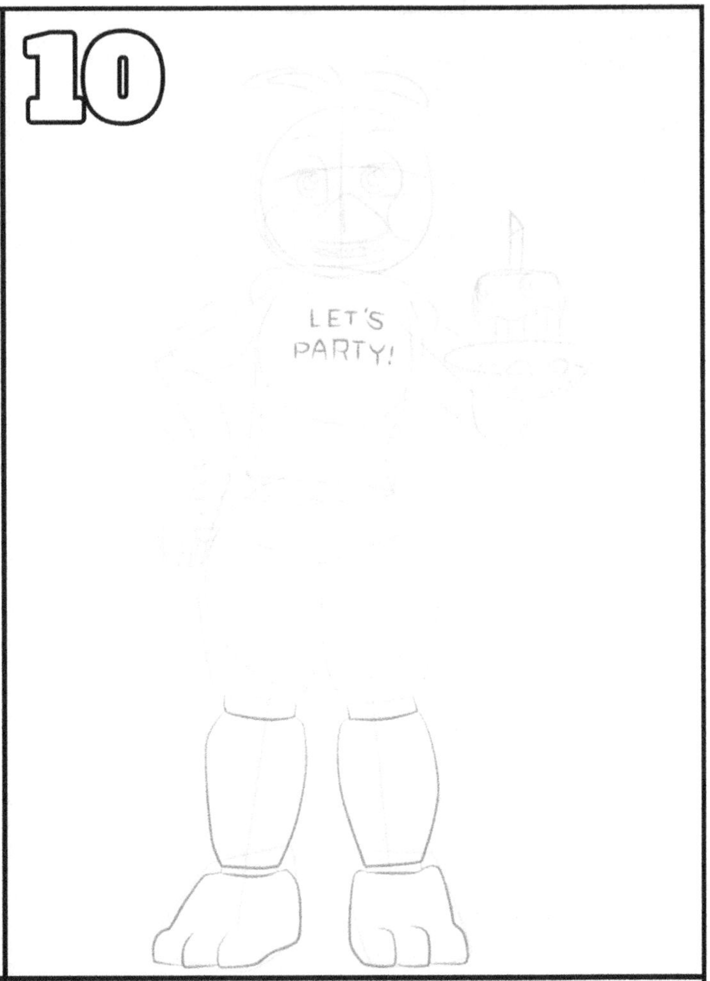
LET'S
PARTY!

11

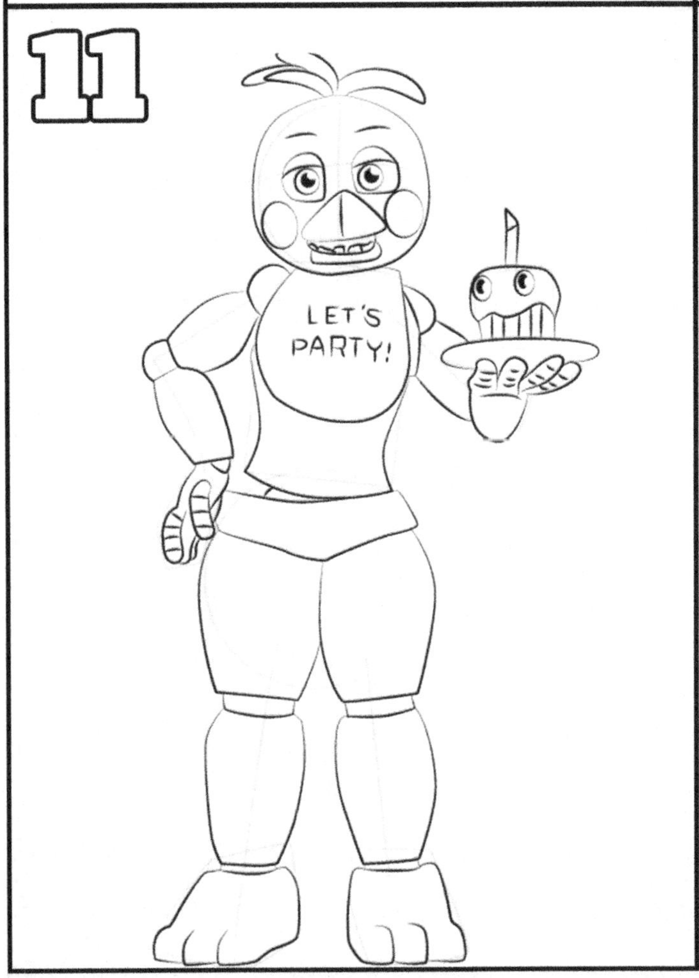
LET'S
PARTY!

12

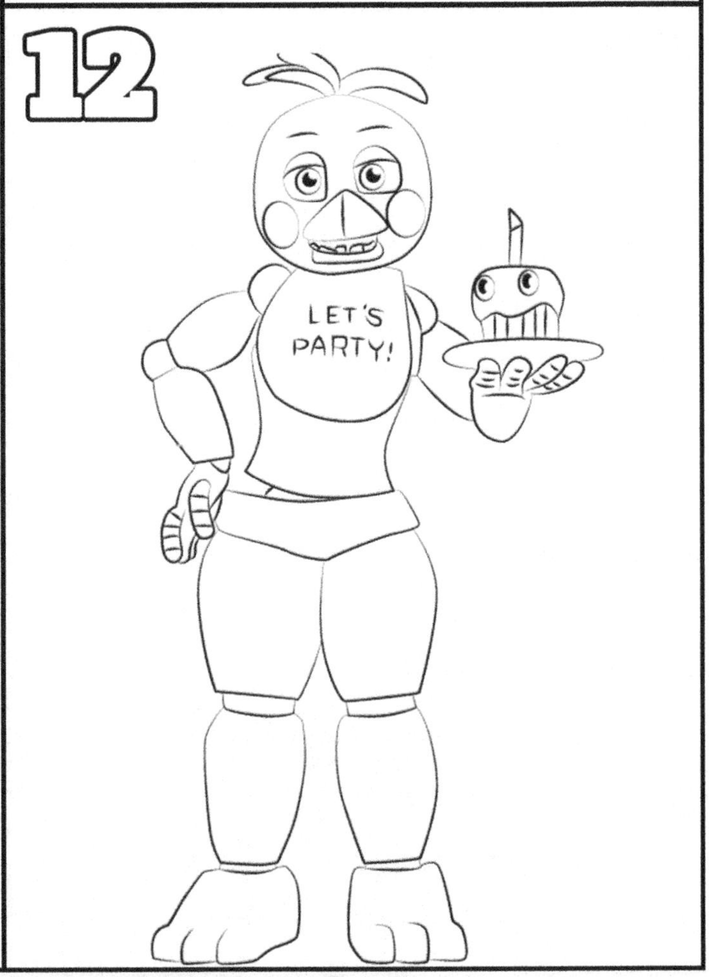
LET'S
PARTY!

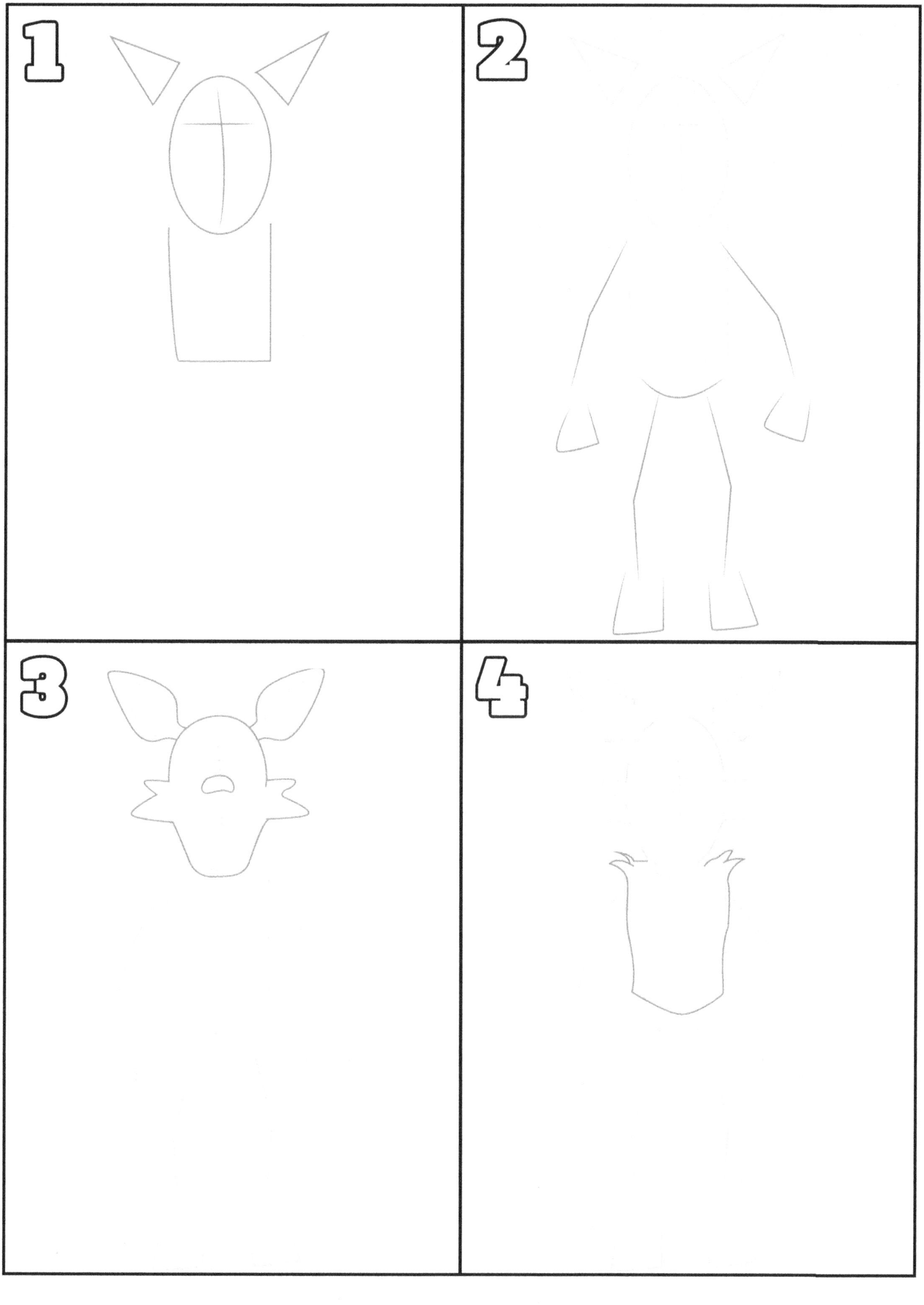
1
2
3
4

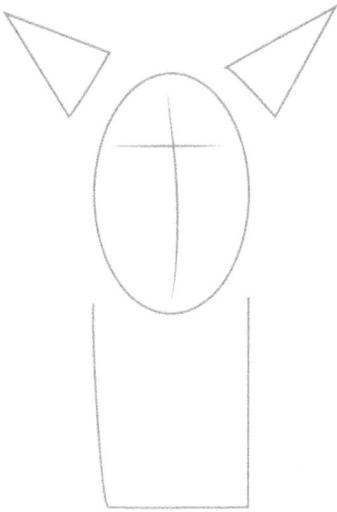

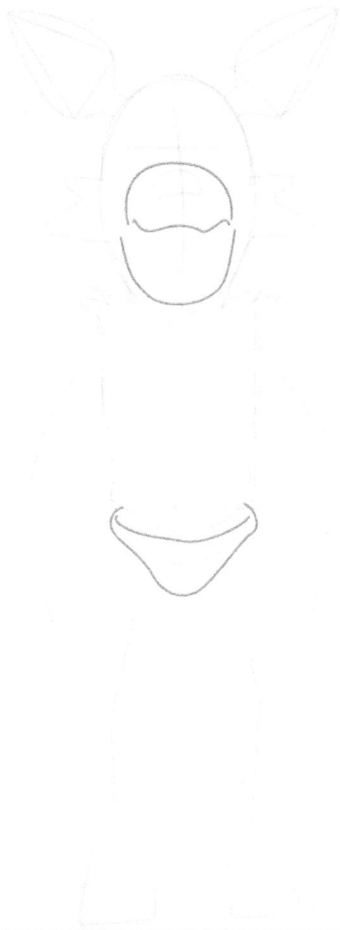

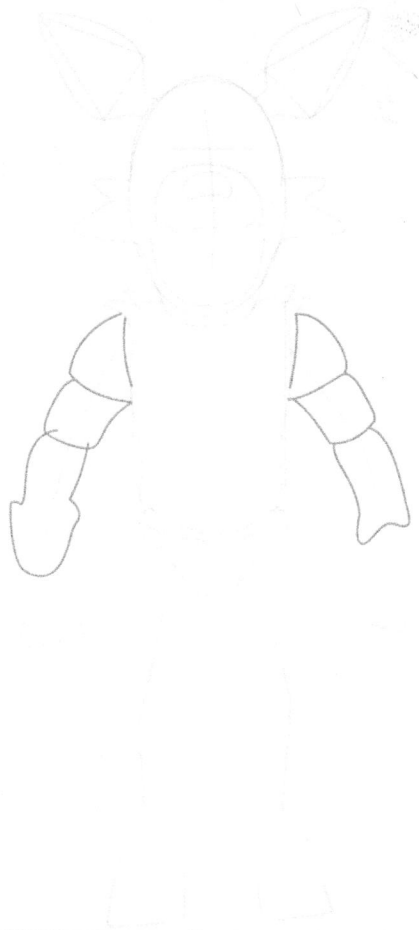

9

10

11

12

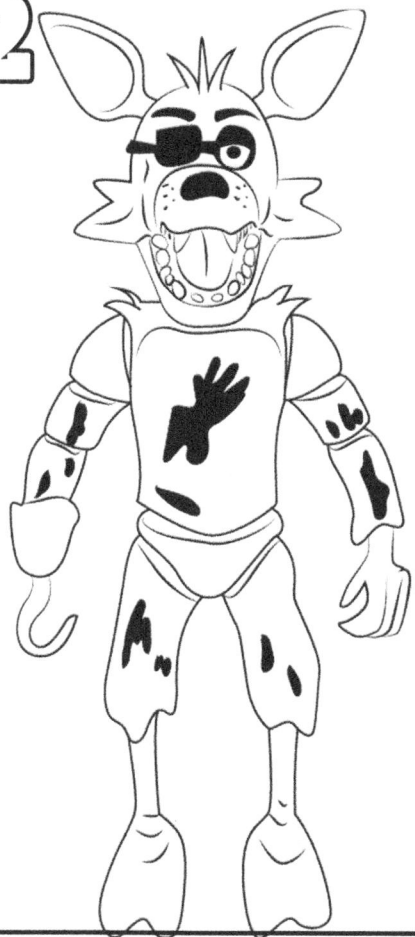

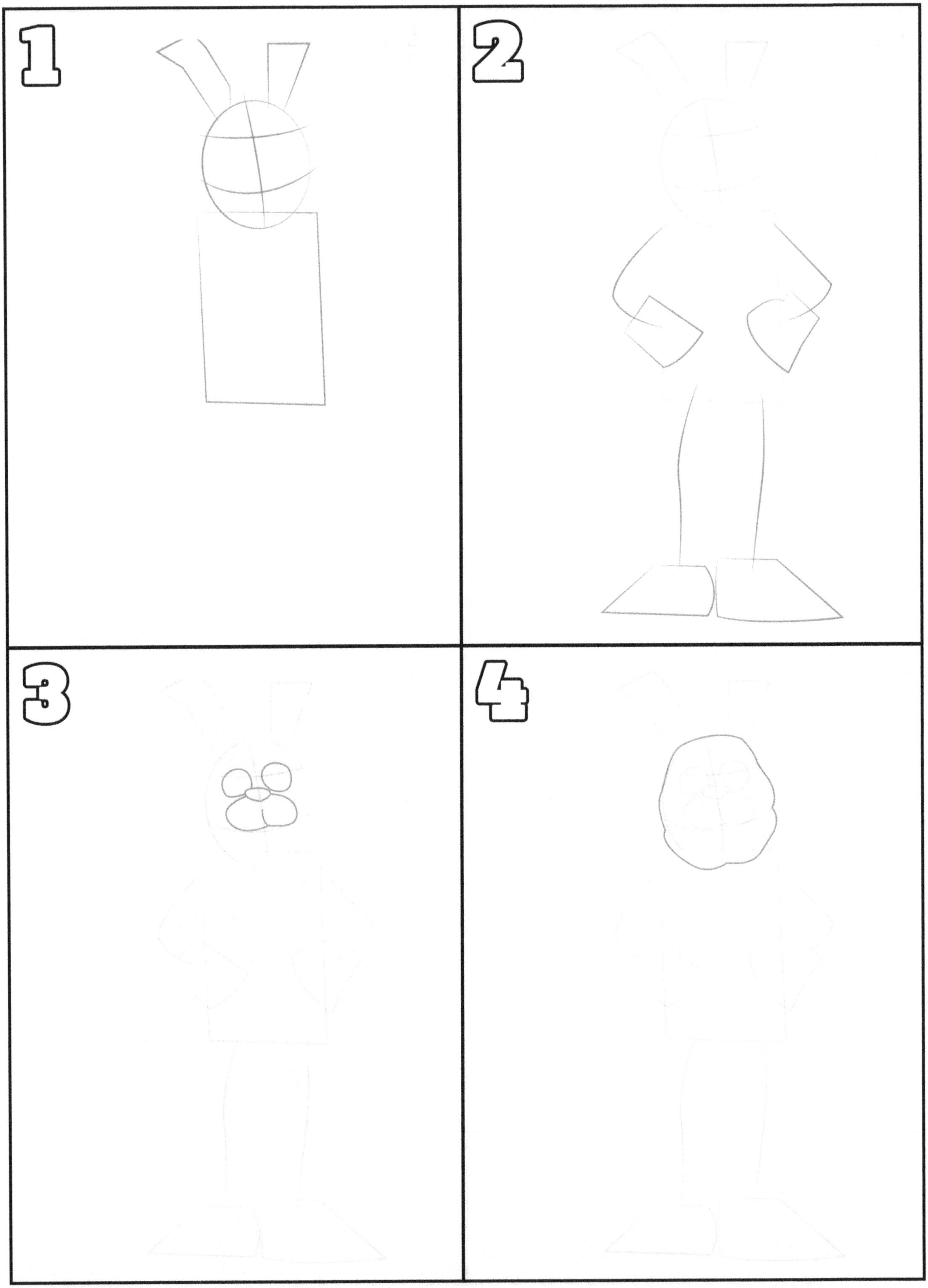
1
2
3
4

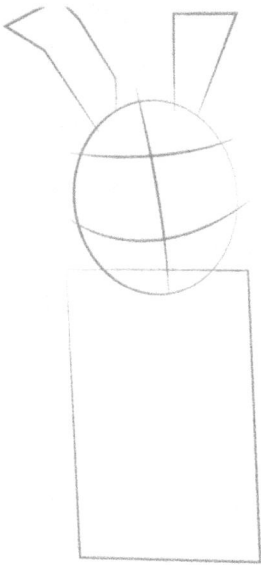

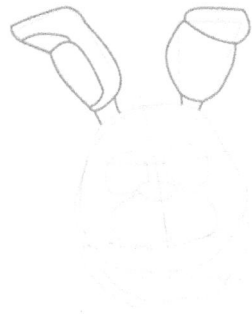

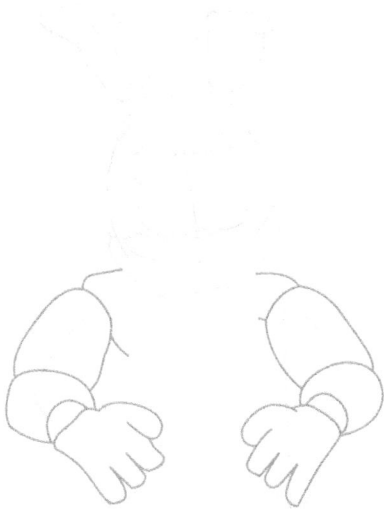

9

10

11

12

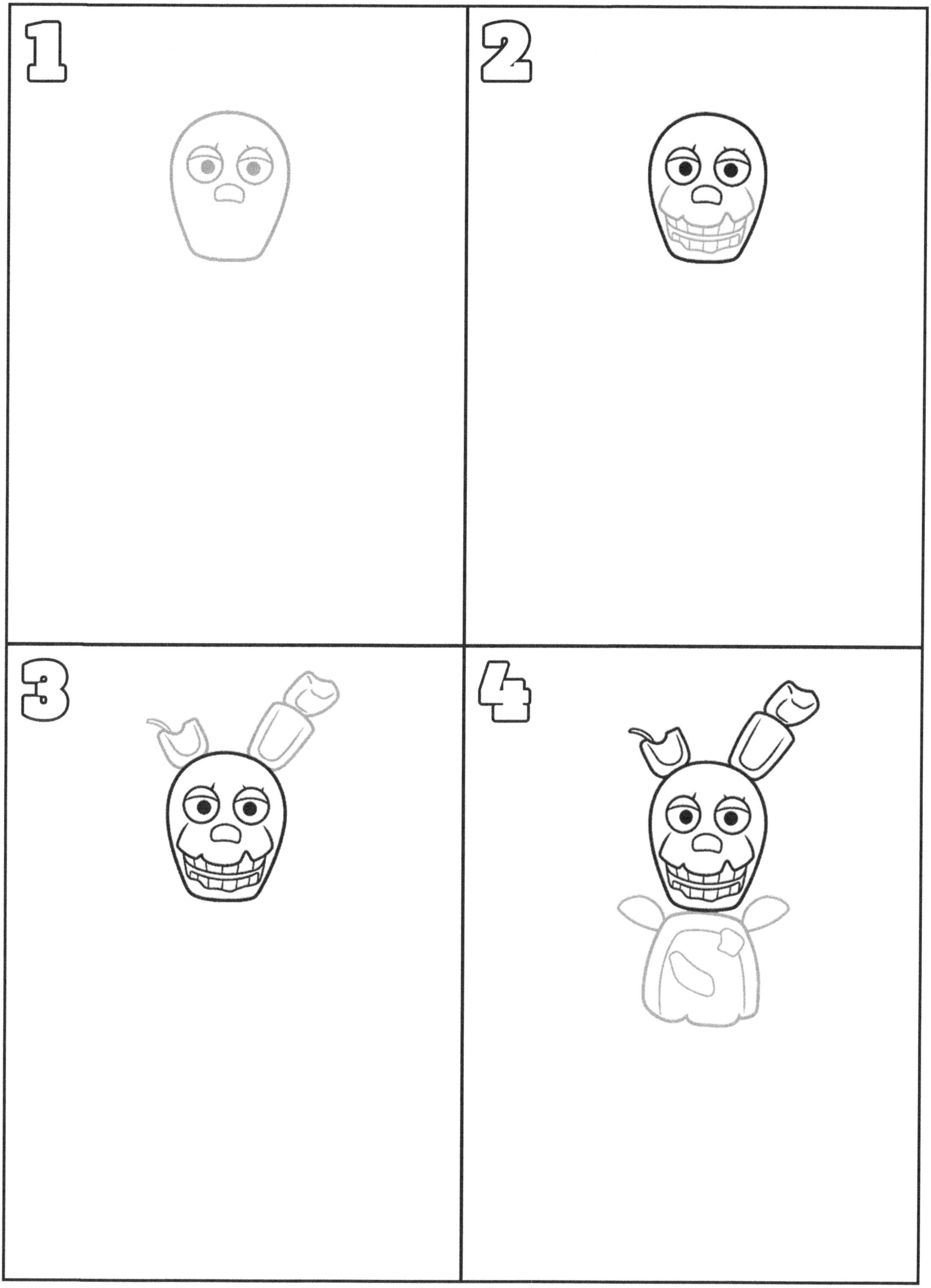
1
2
3
4

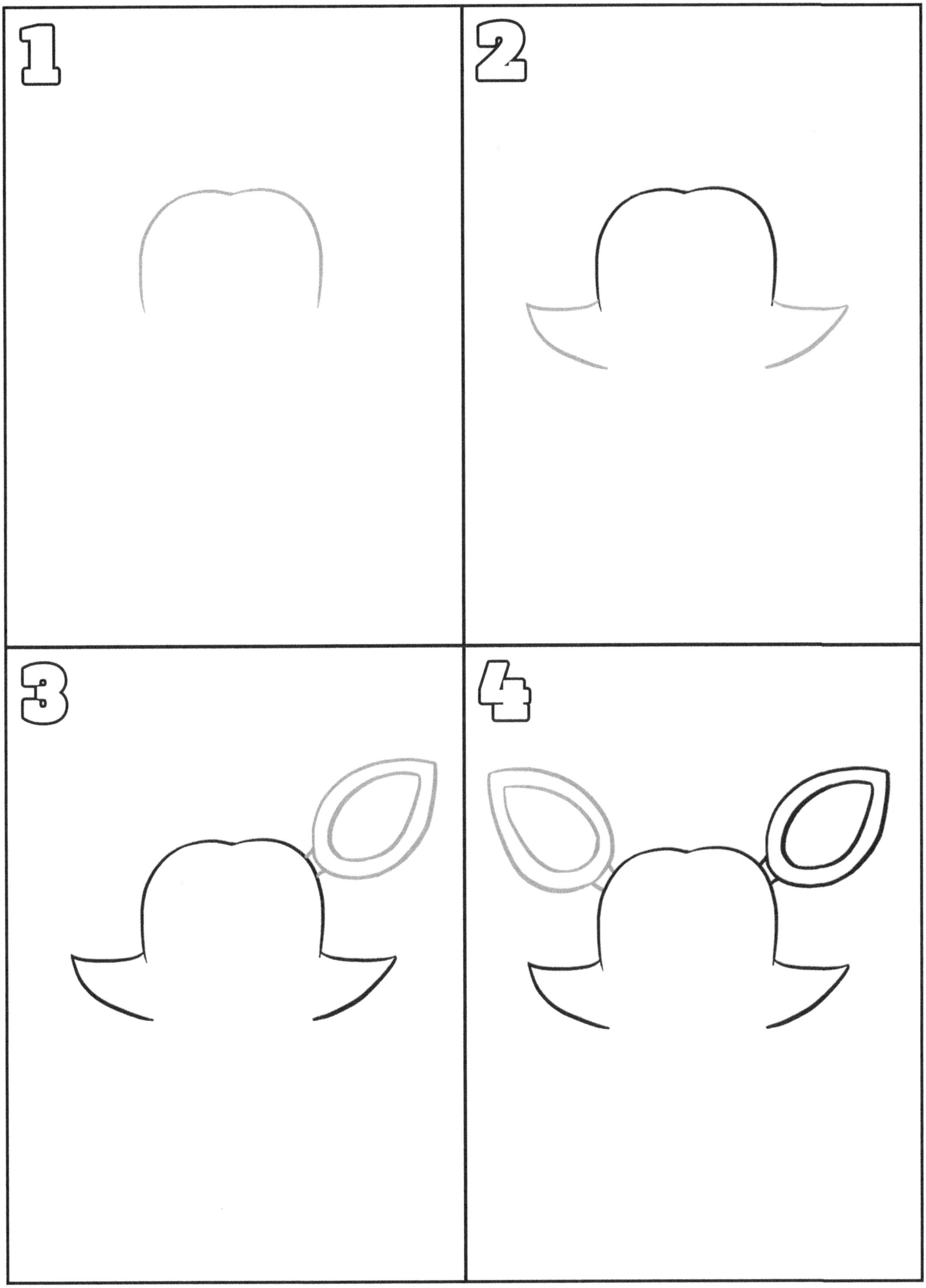
1
2
3
4

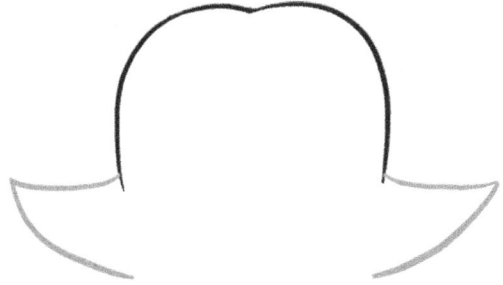

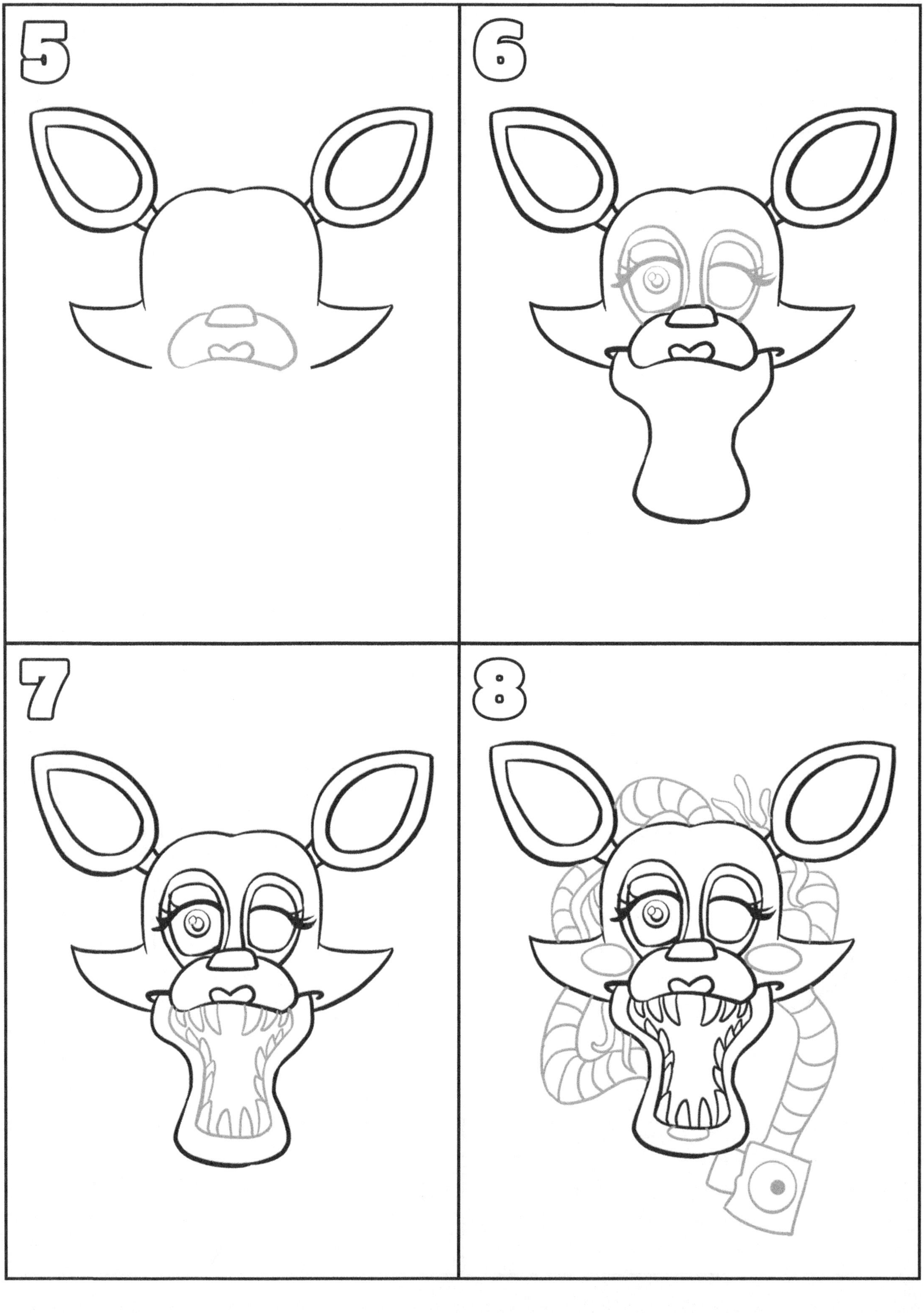
5
6
7
8

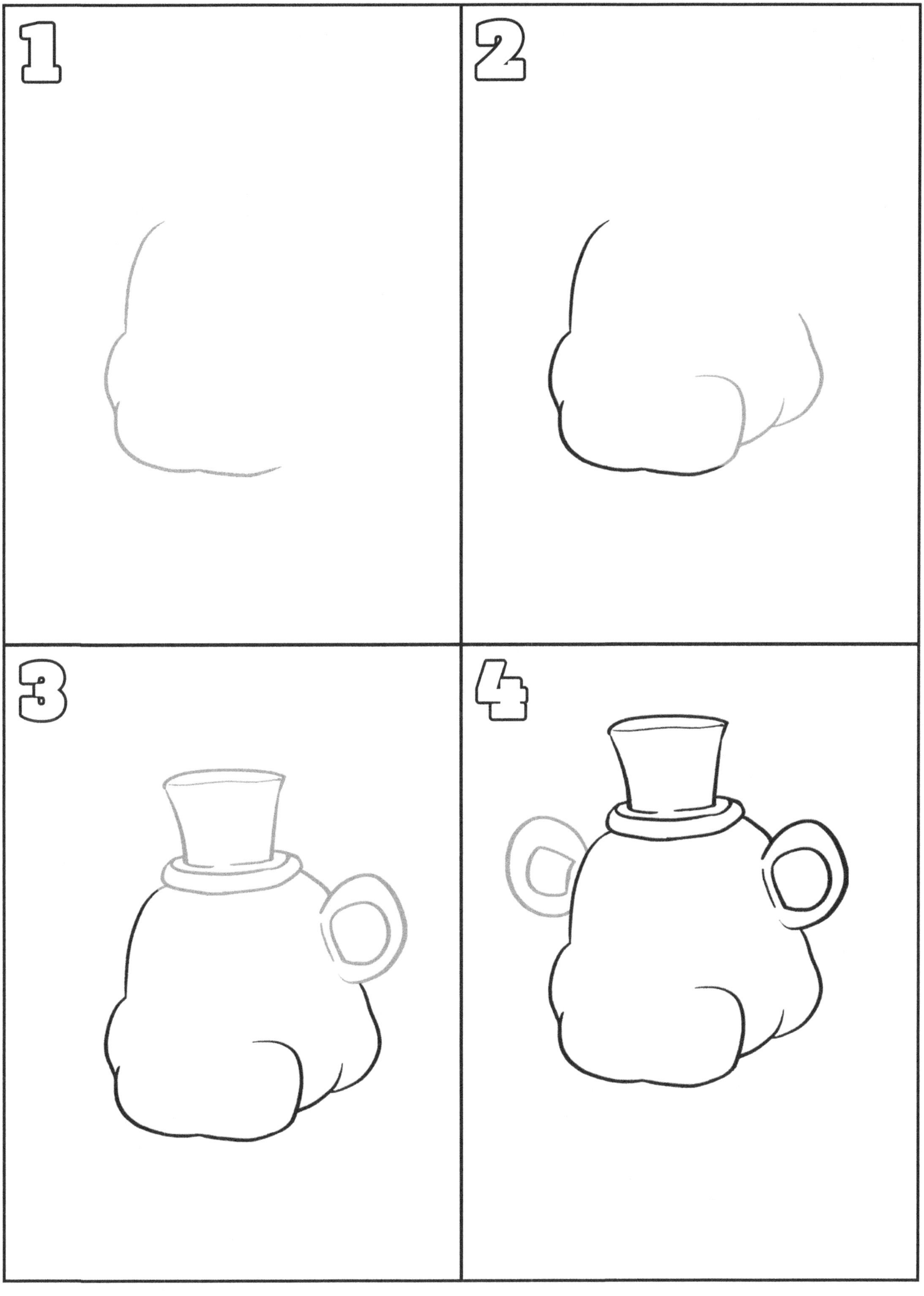
1
2
3
4

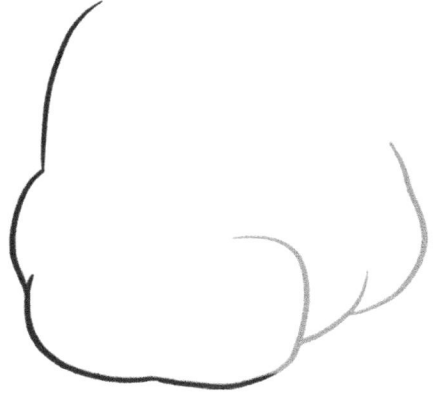

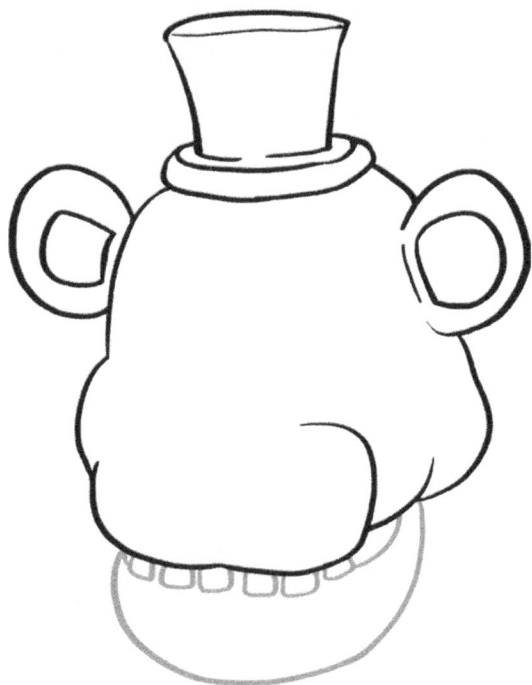

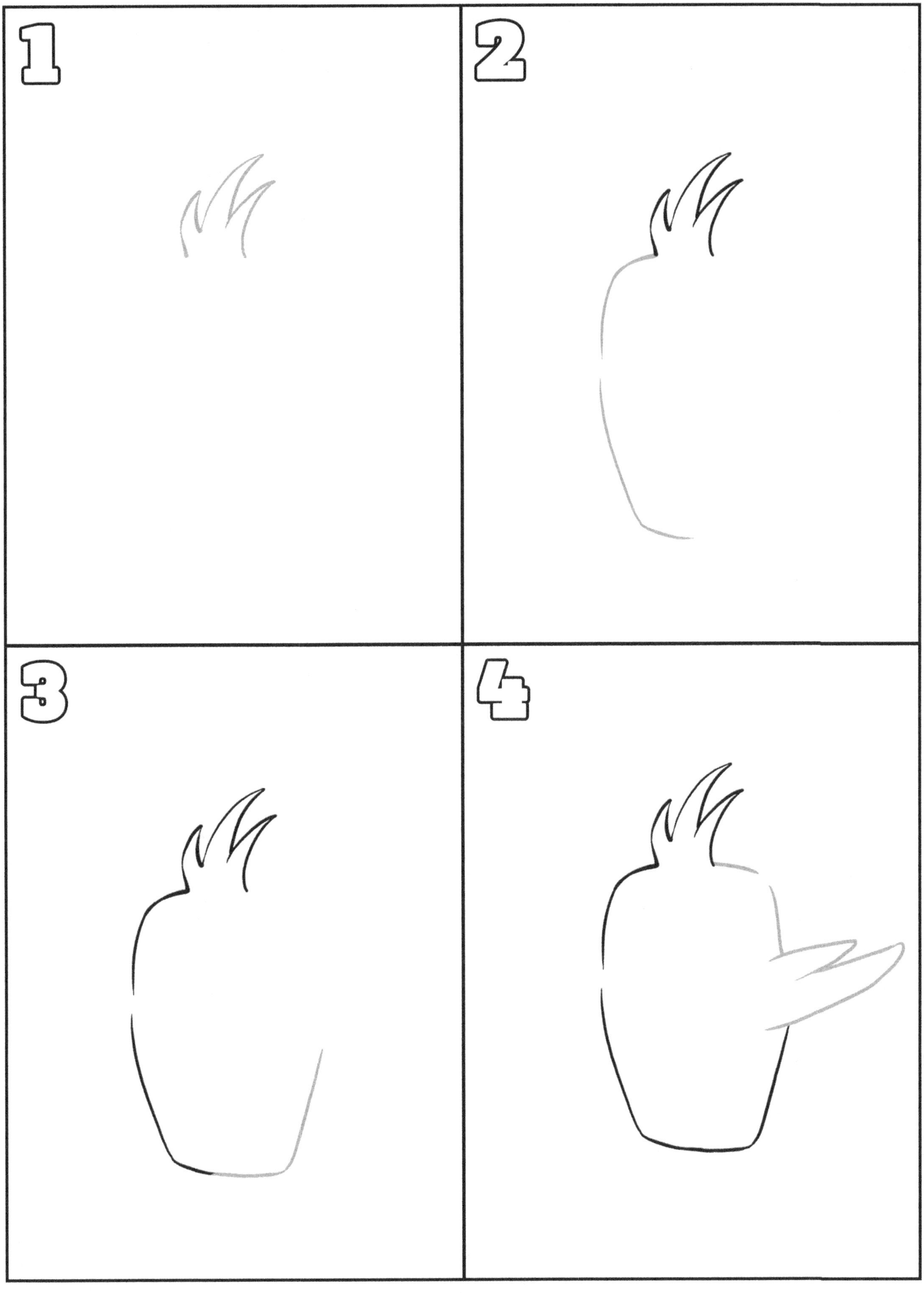
1
2
3
4

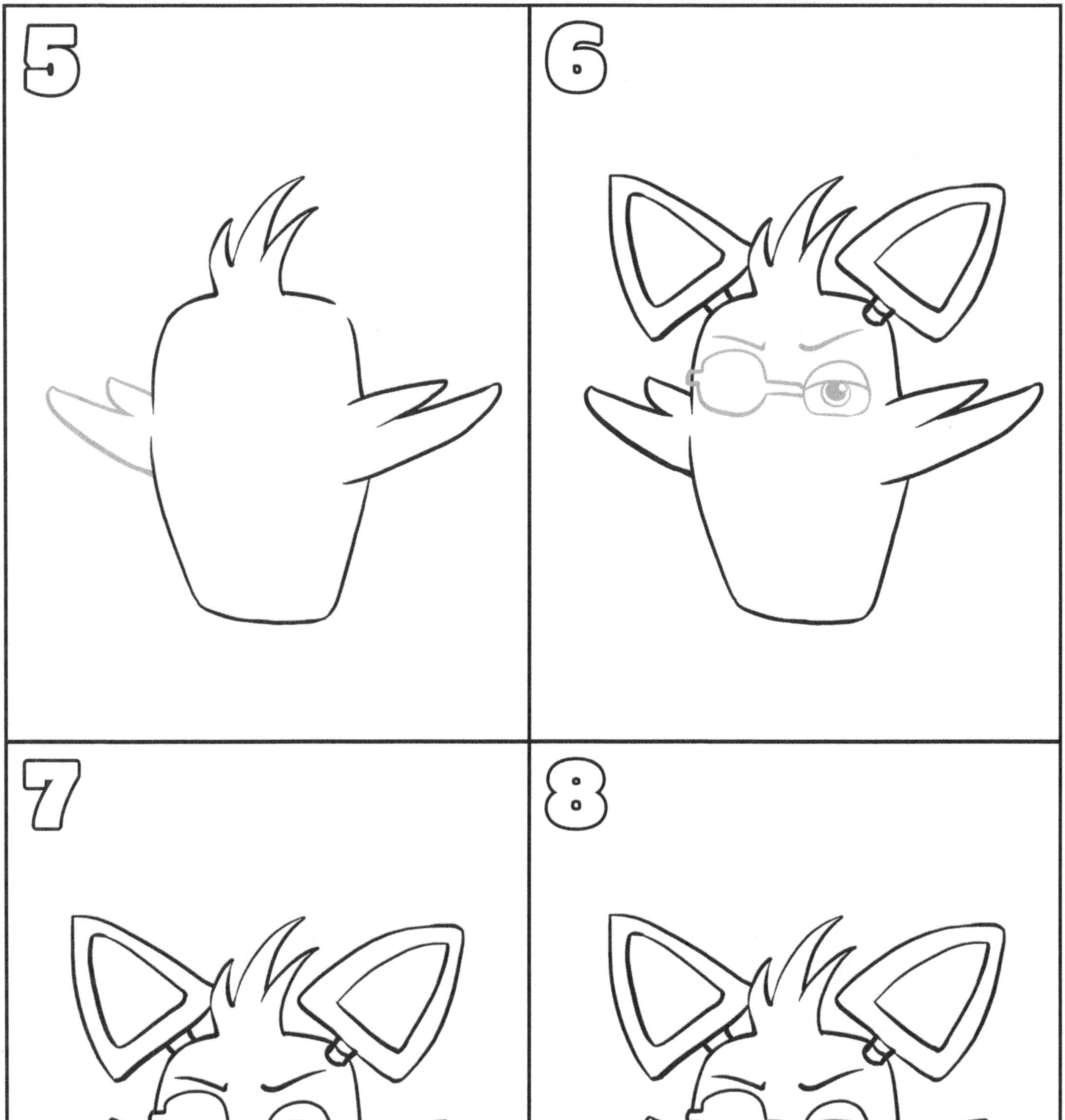
5
6
7
8

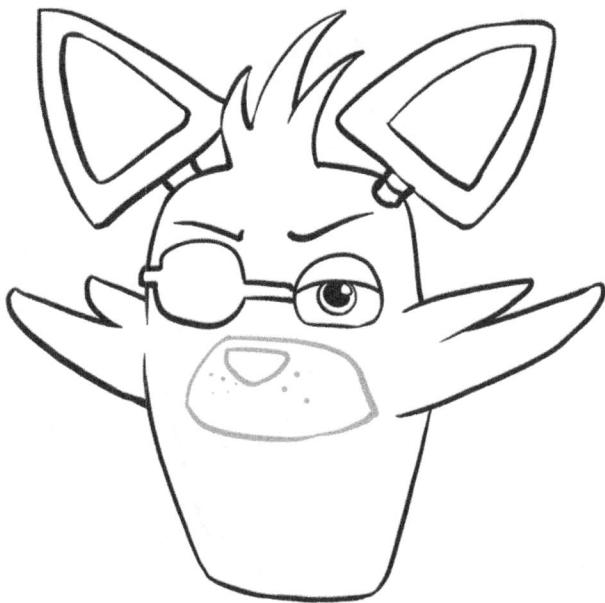

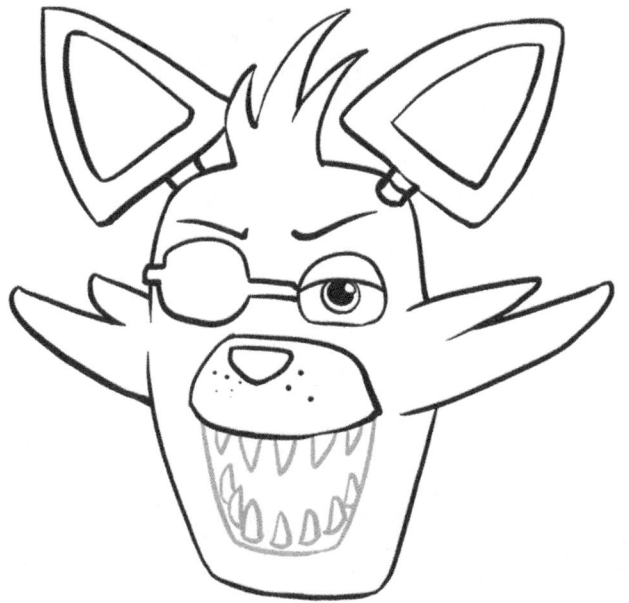

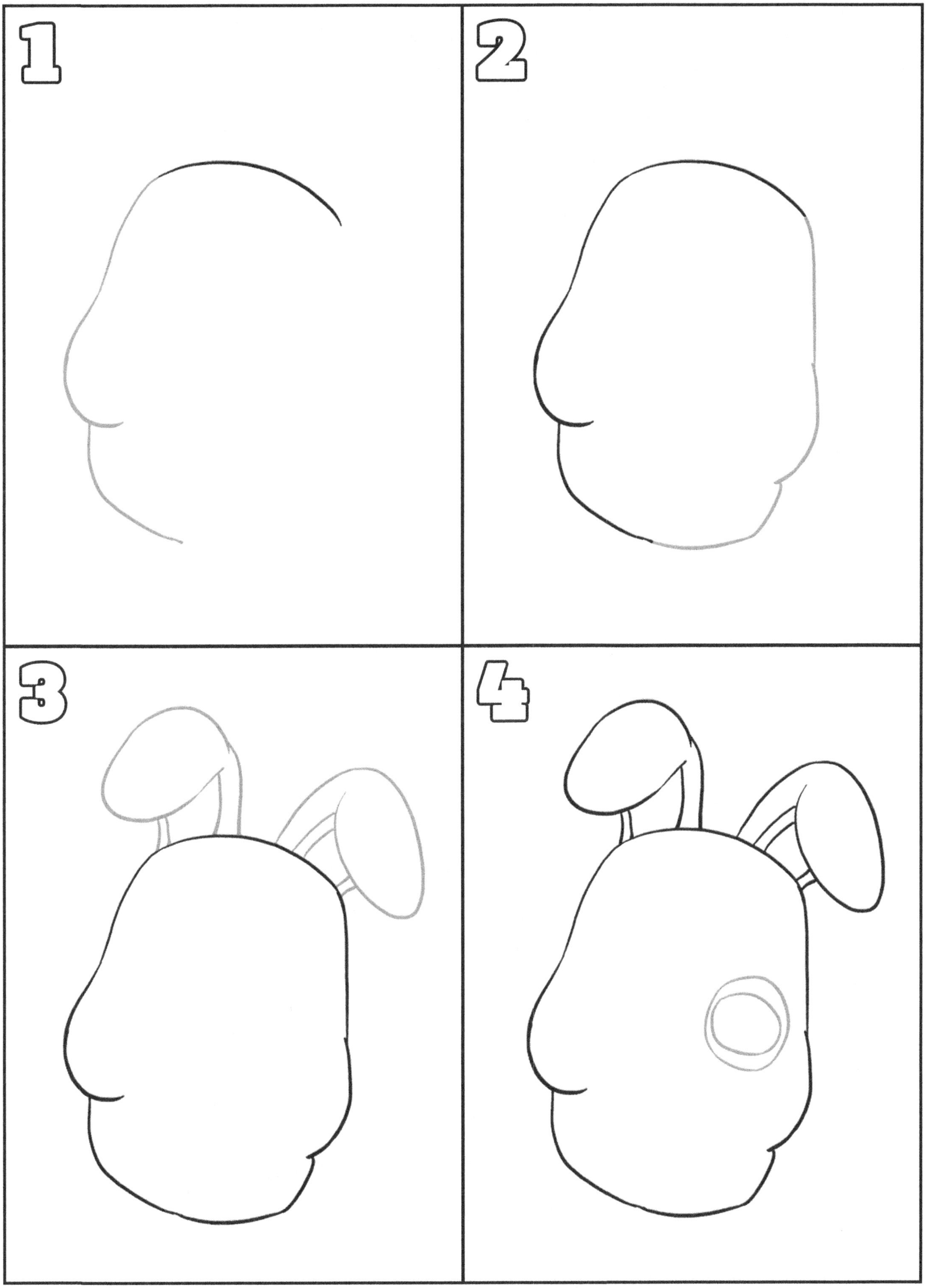
1
2
3
4

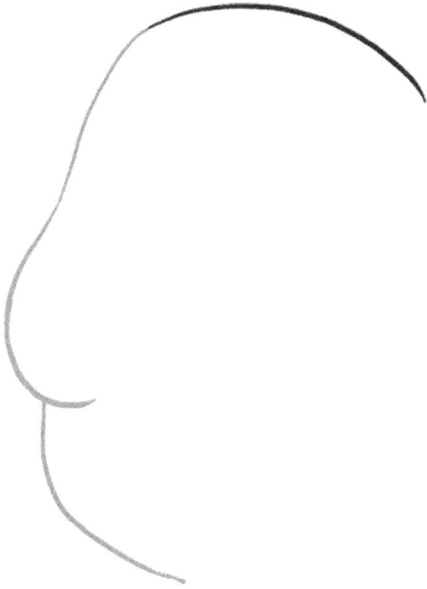

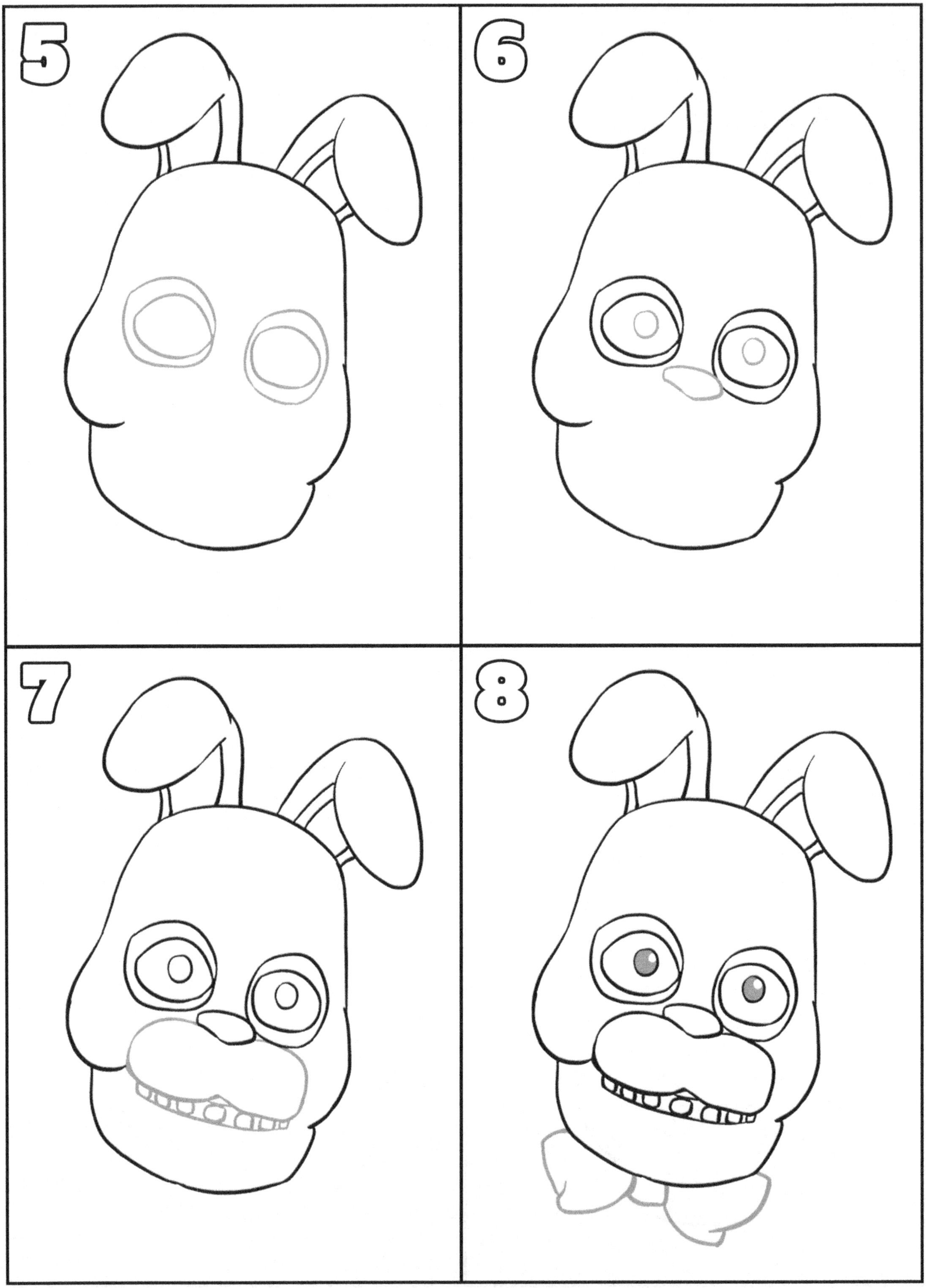
5
6
7
8

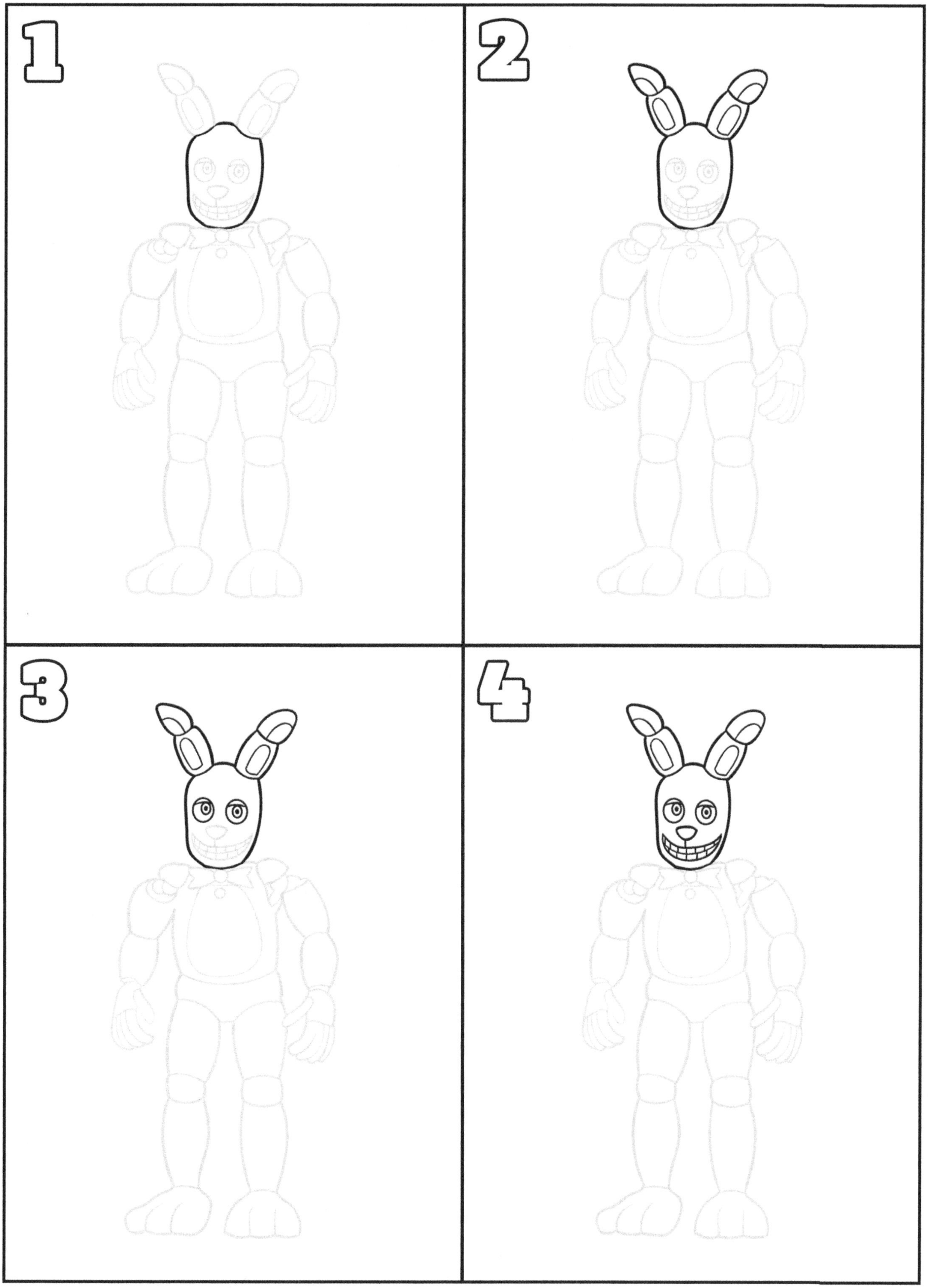
1
2
3
4

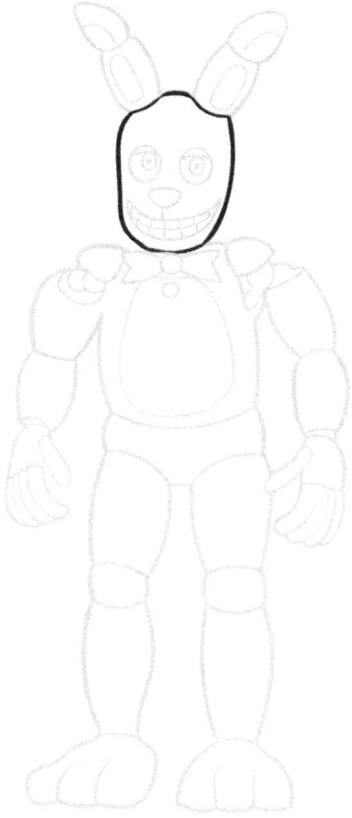

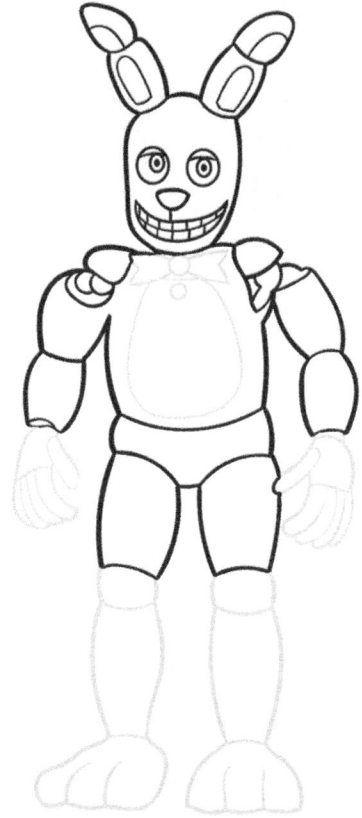

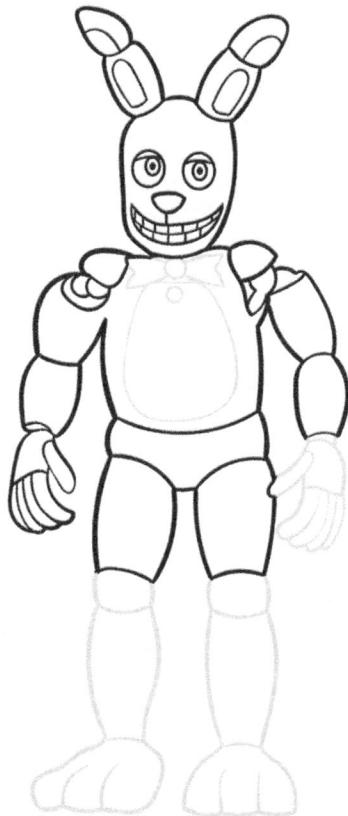

9

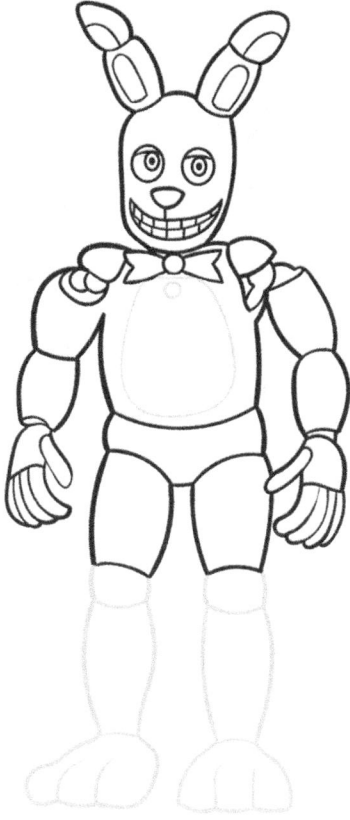

10

11

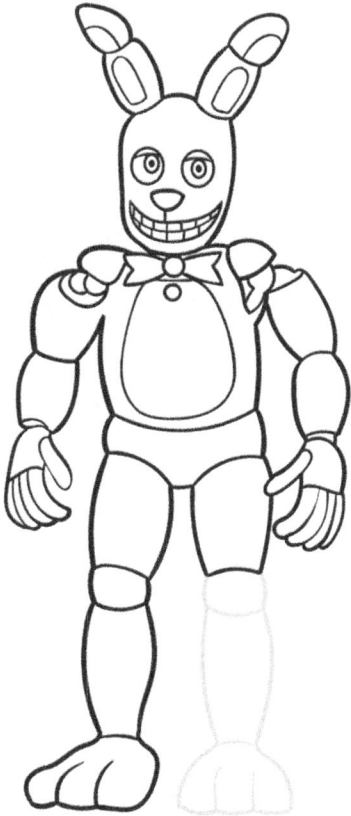

12

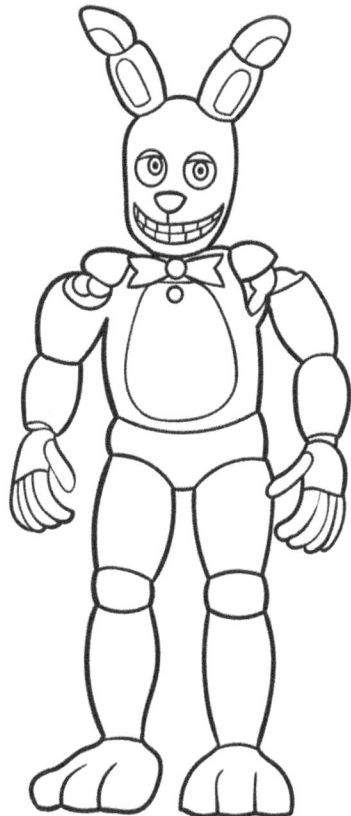

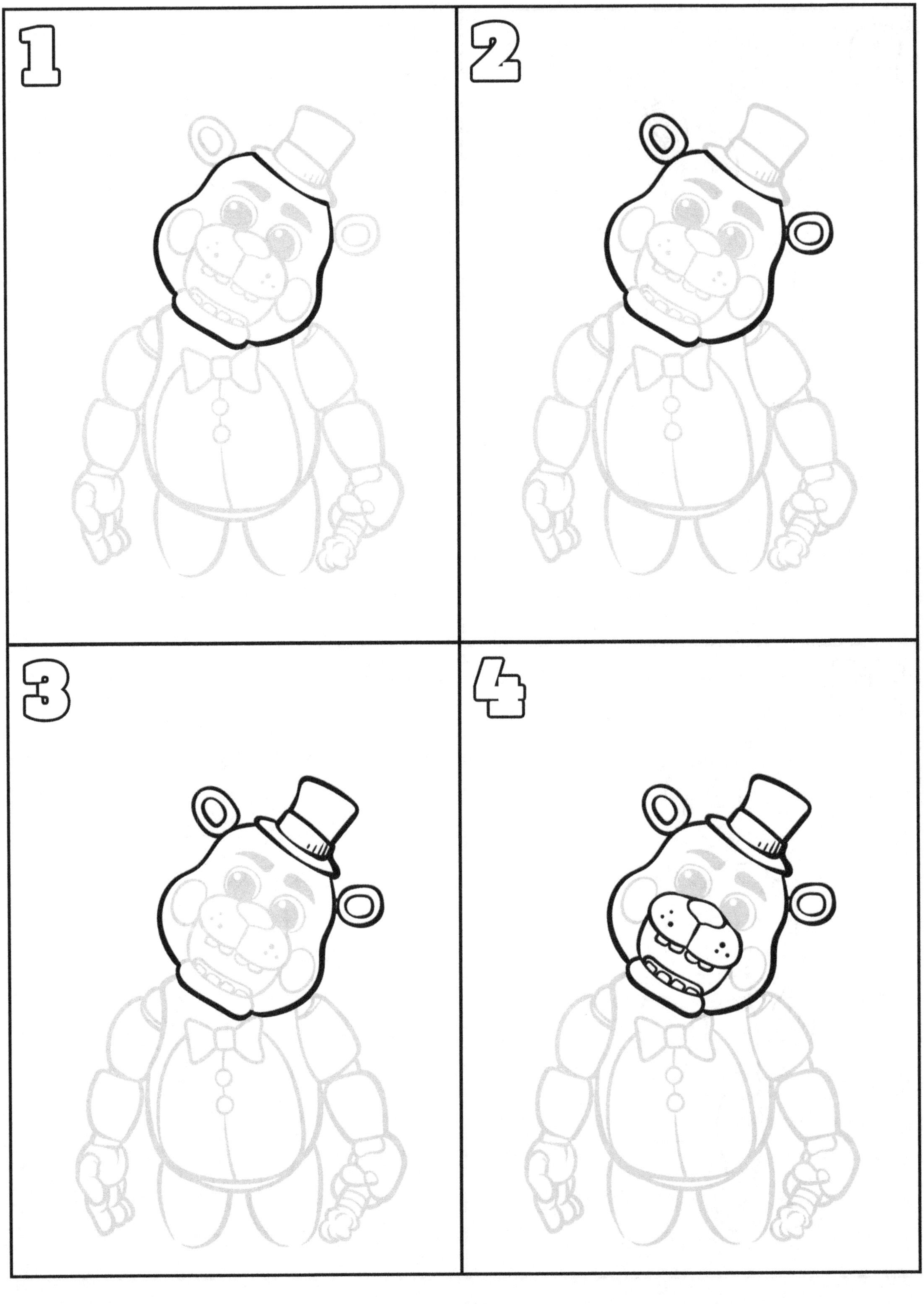
1
2
3
4

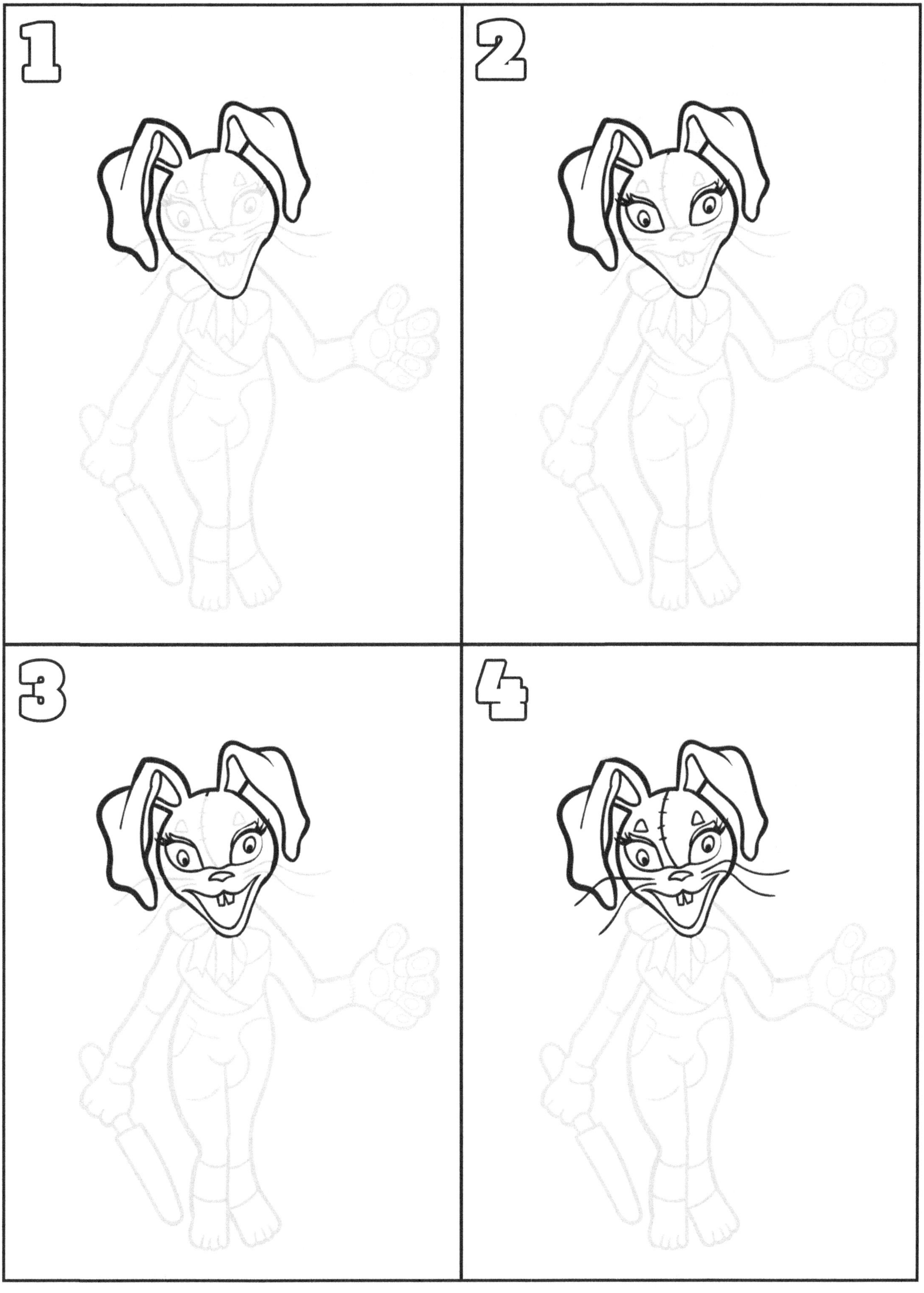
1
2
3
4

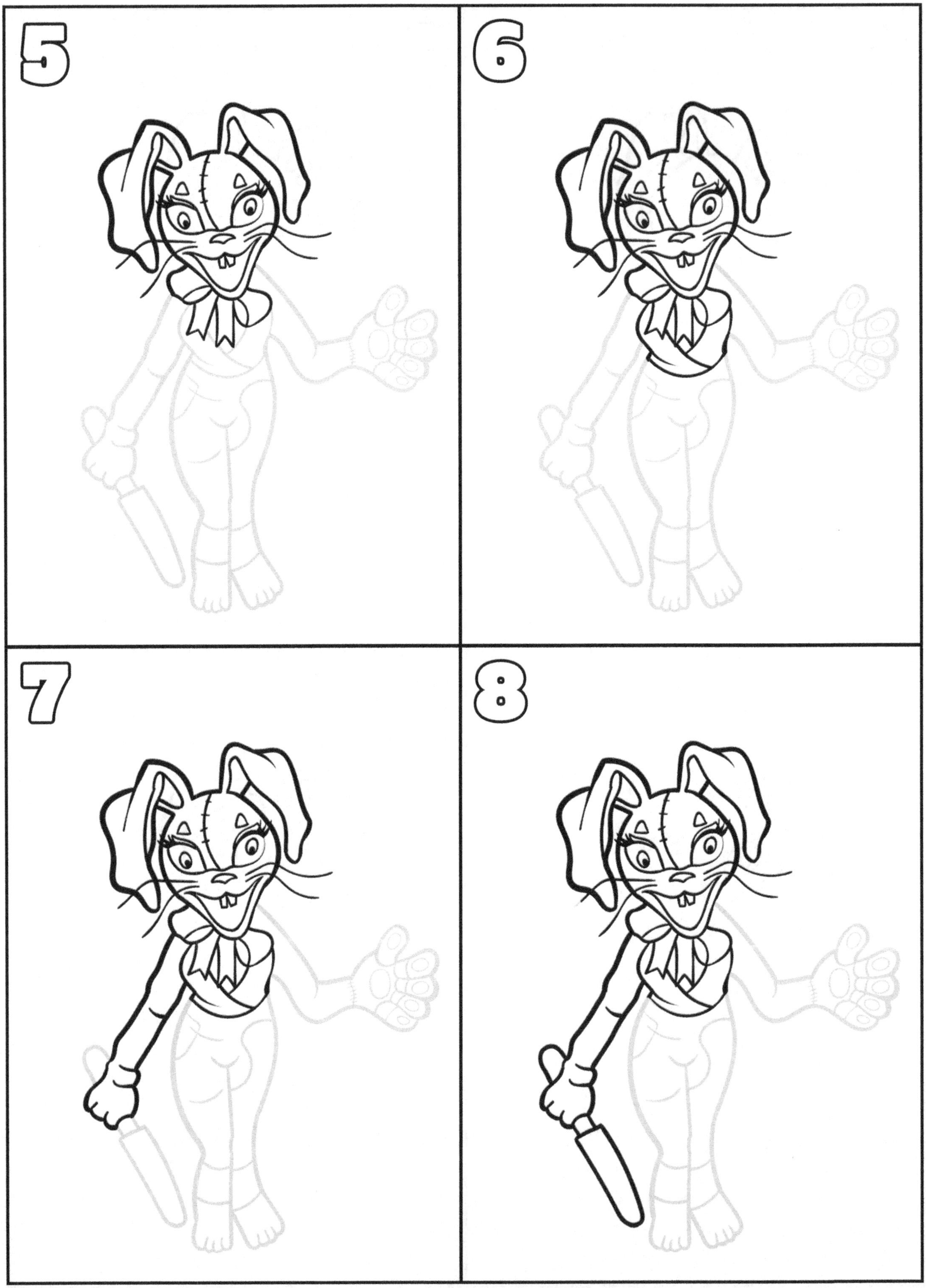
5
6
7
8

9

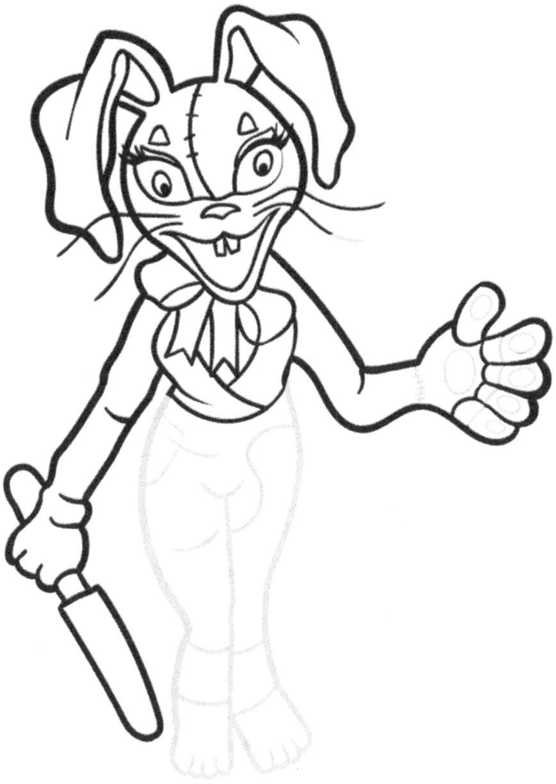

10

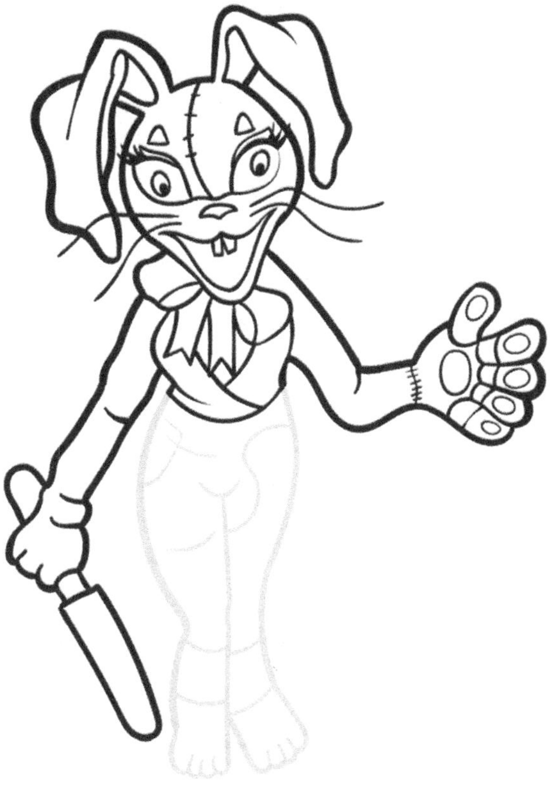

11

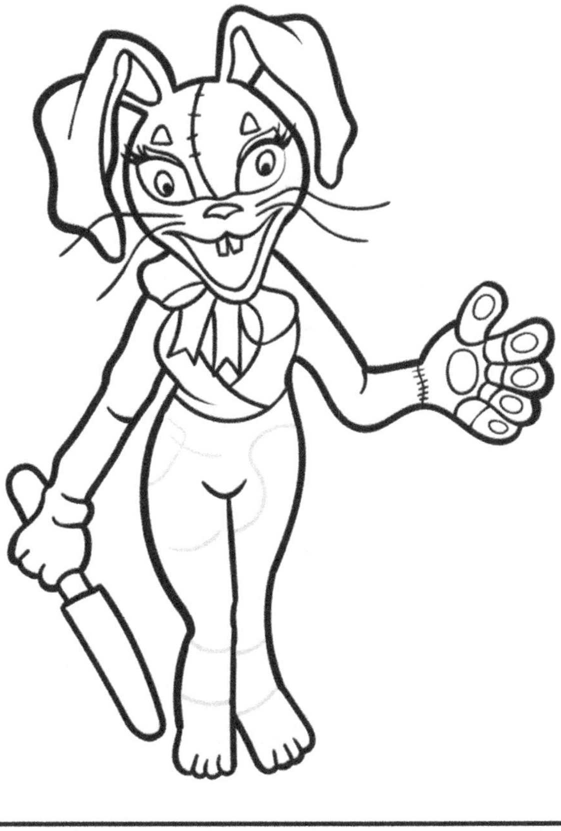

12

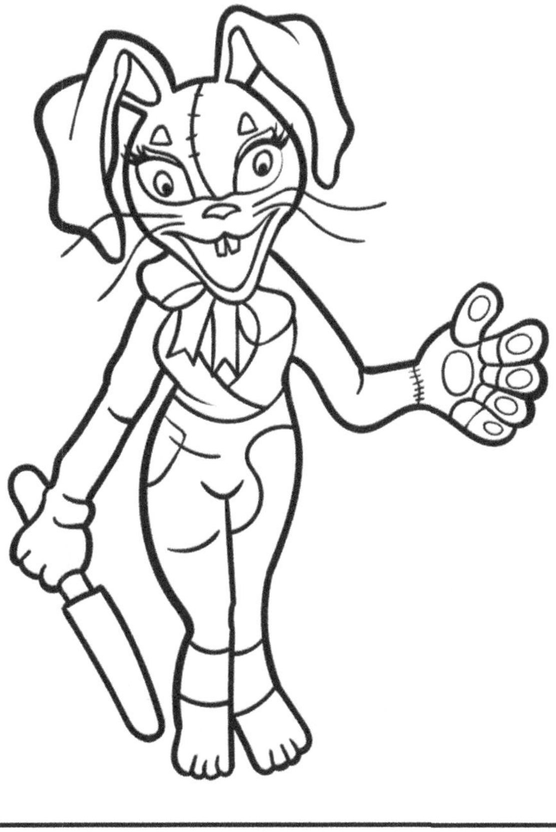

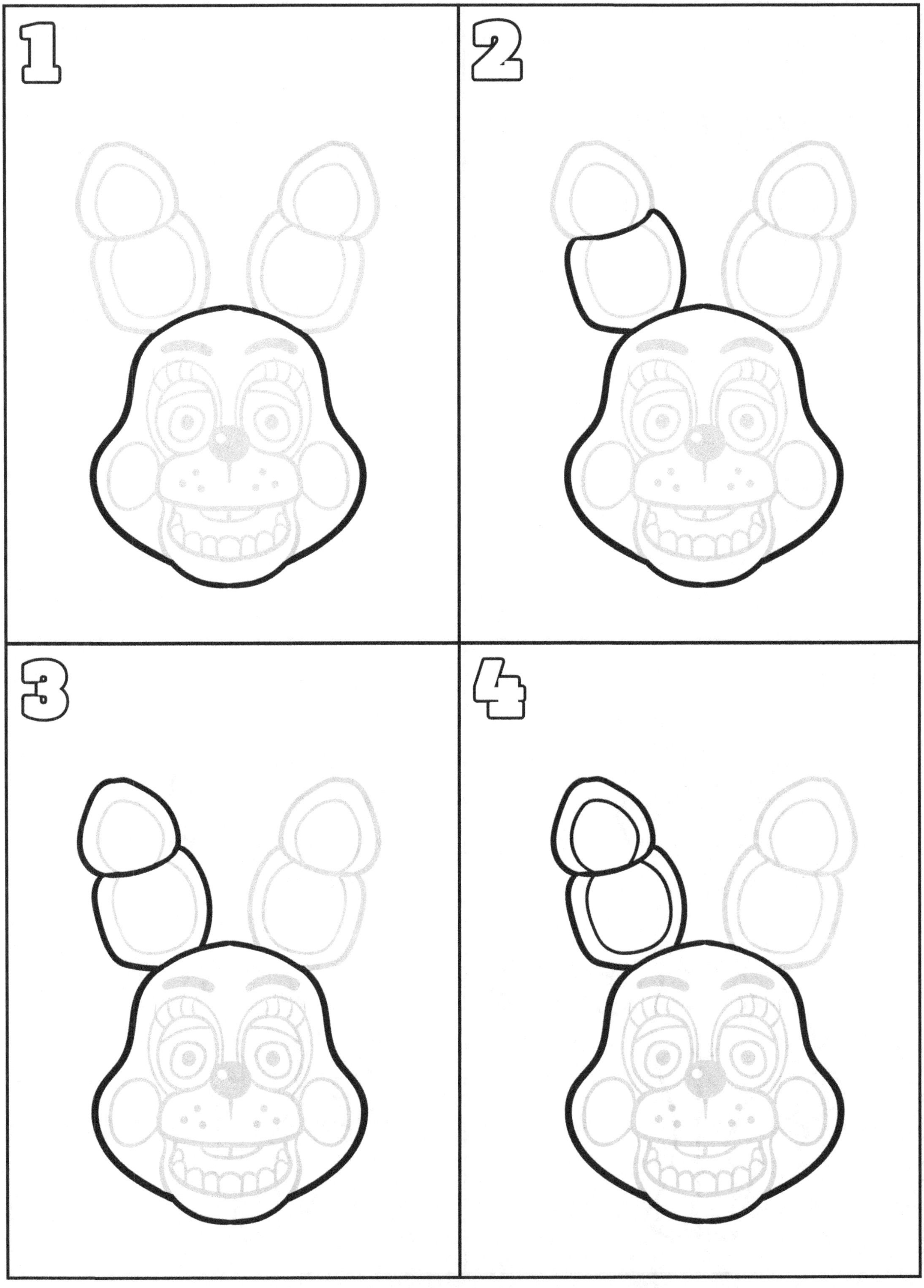
1
2
3
4

5

6

7

8

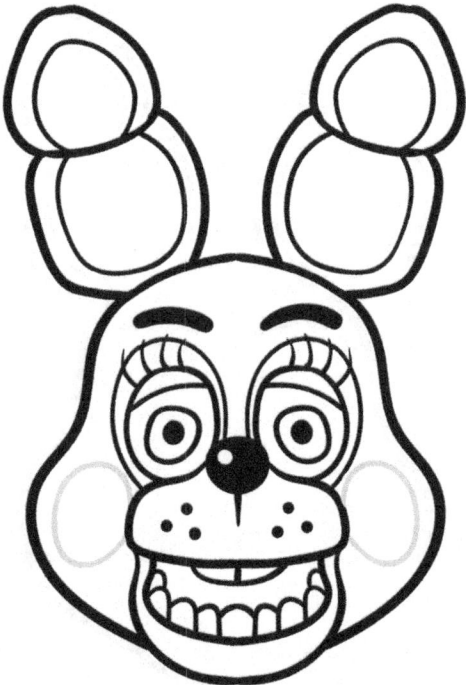

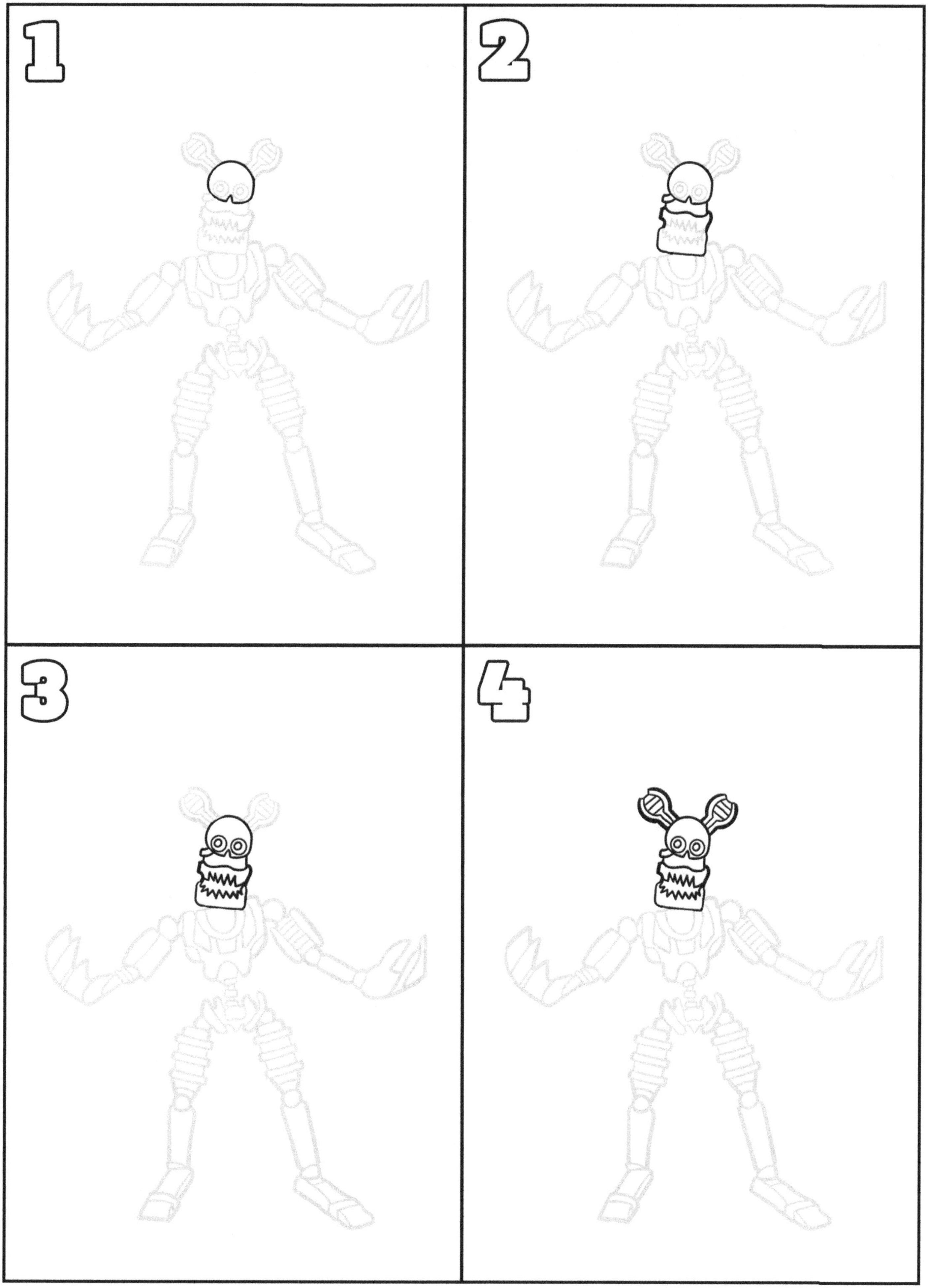
1
2
3
4

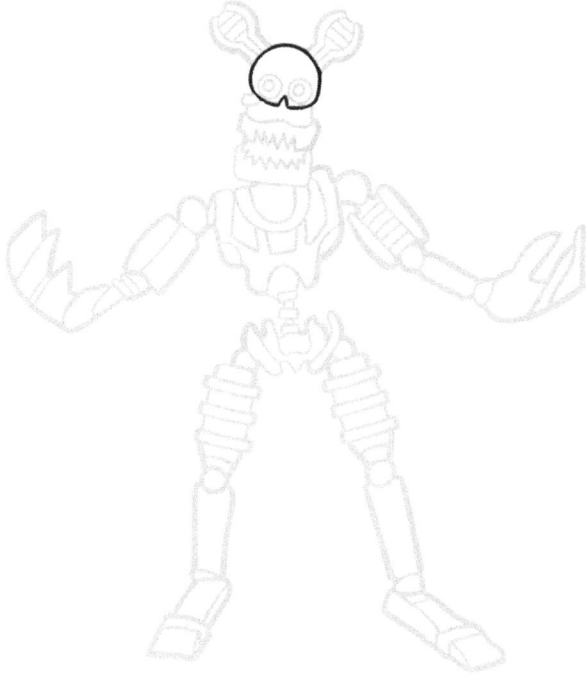

5

6

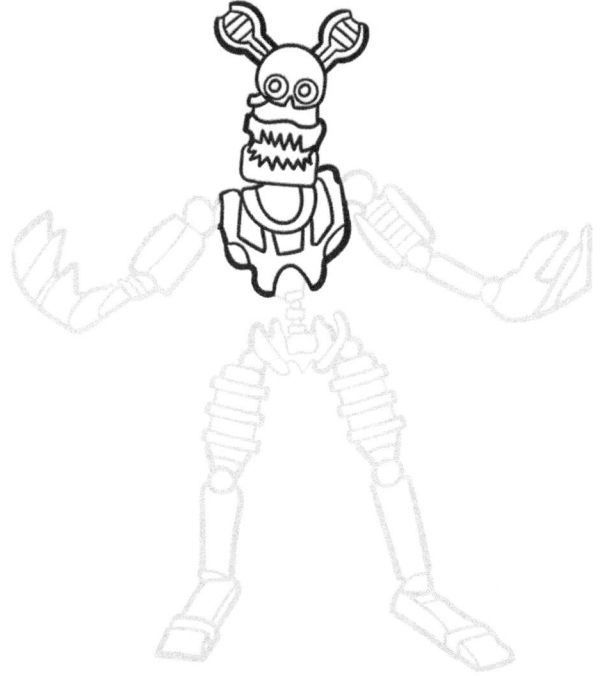

7

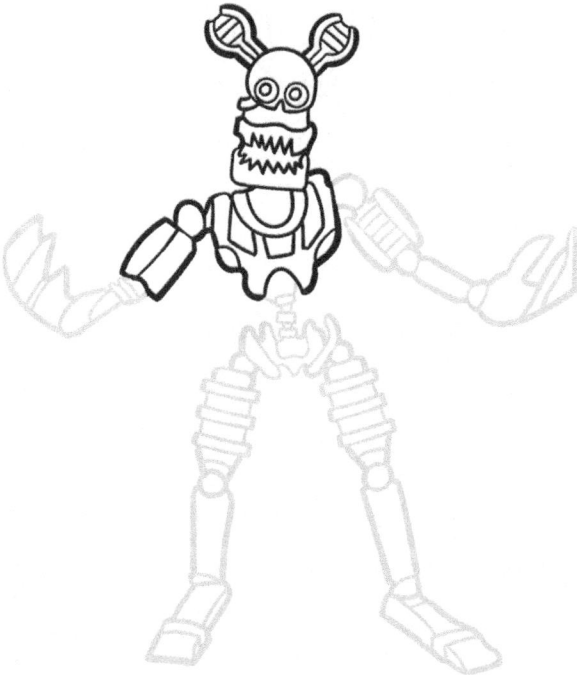

8

9

10

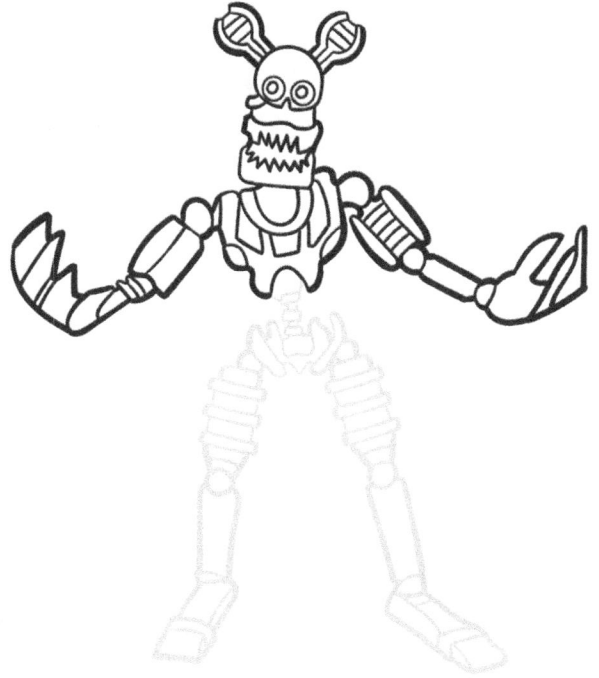

11

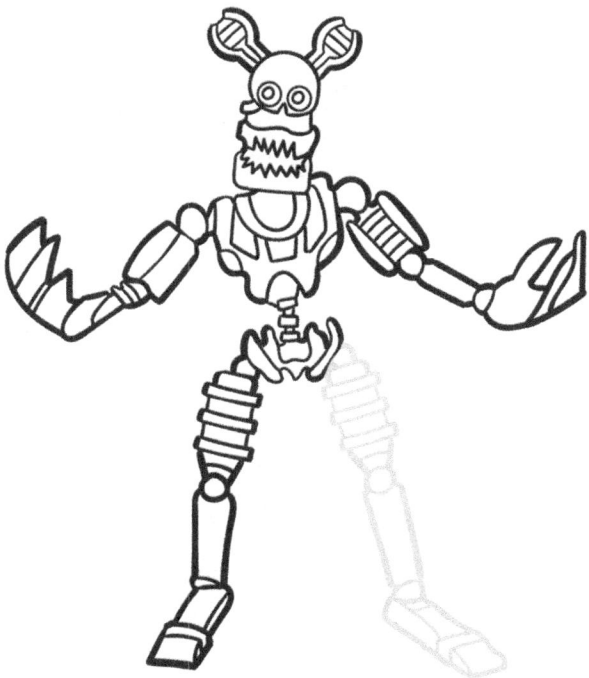

12

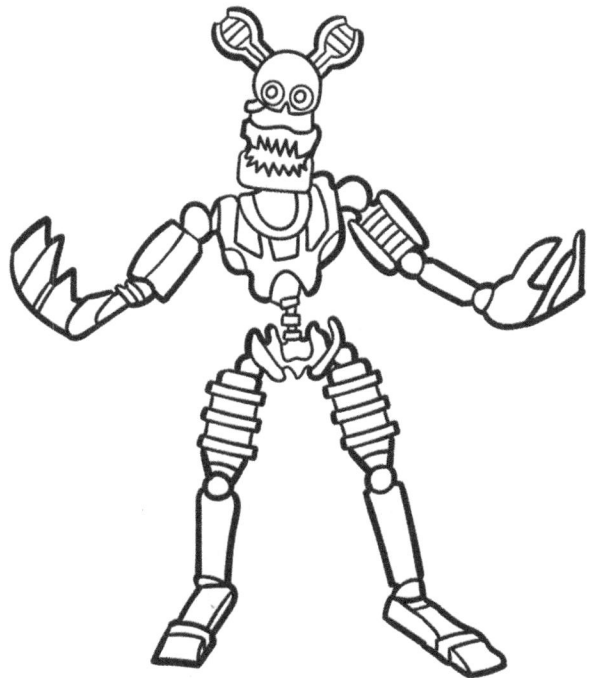

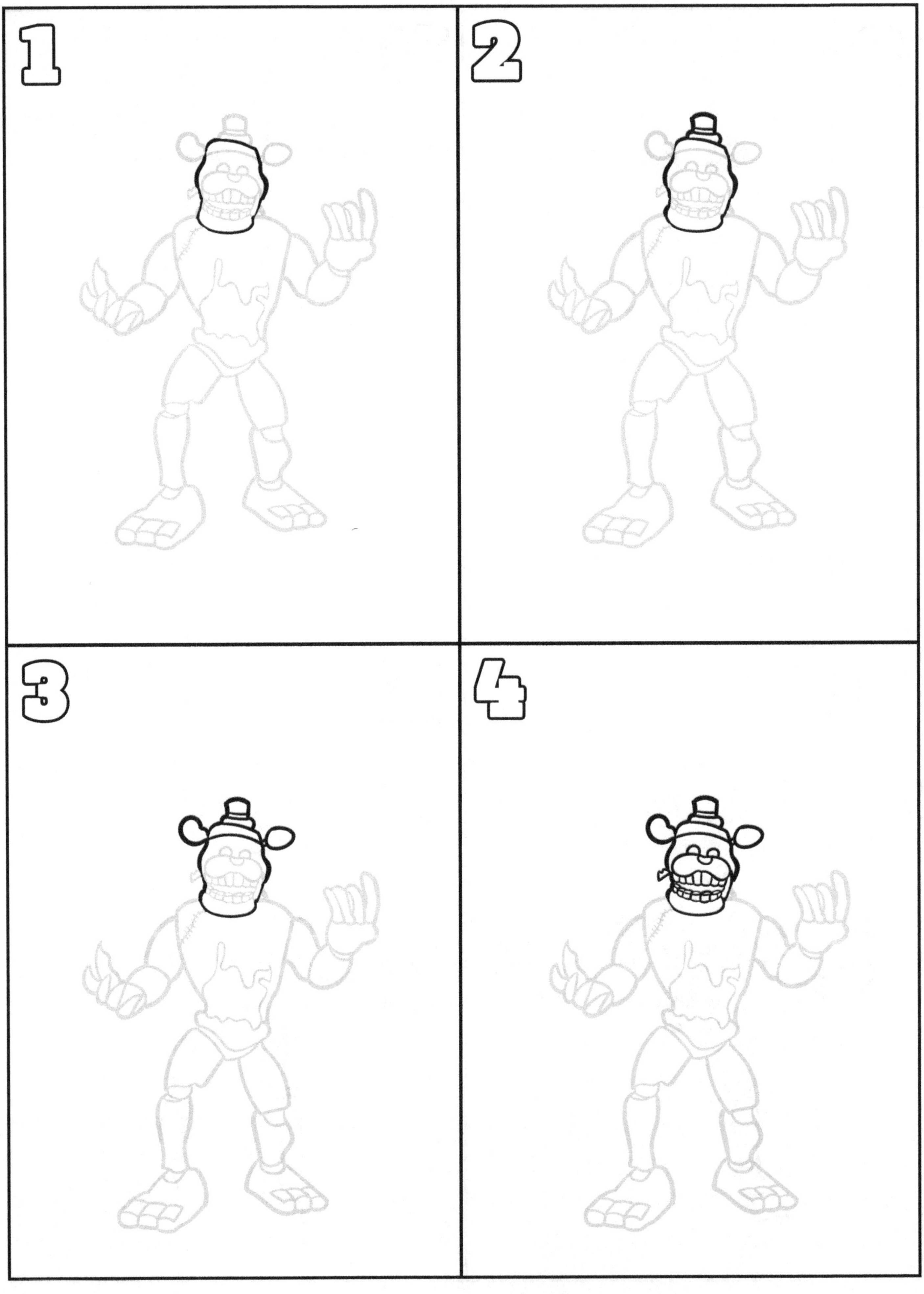
1
2
3
4

9

10

11

12

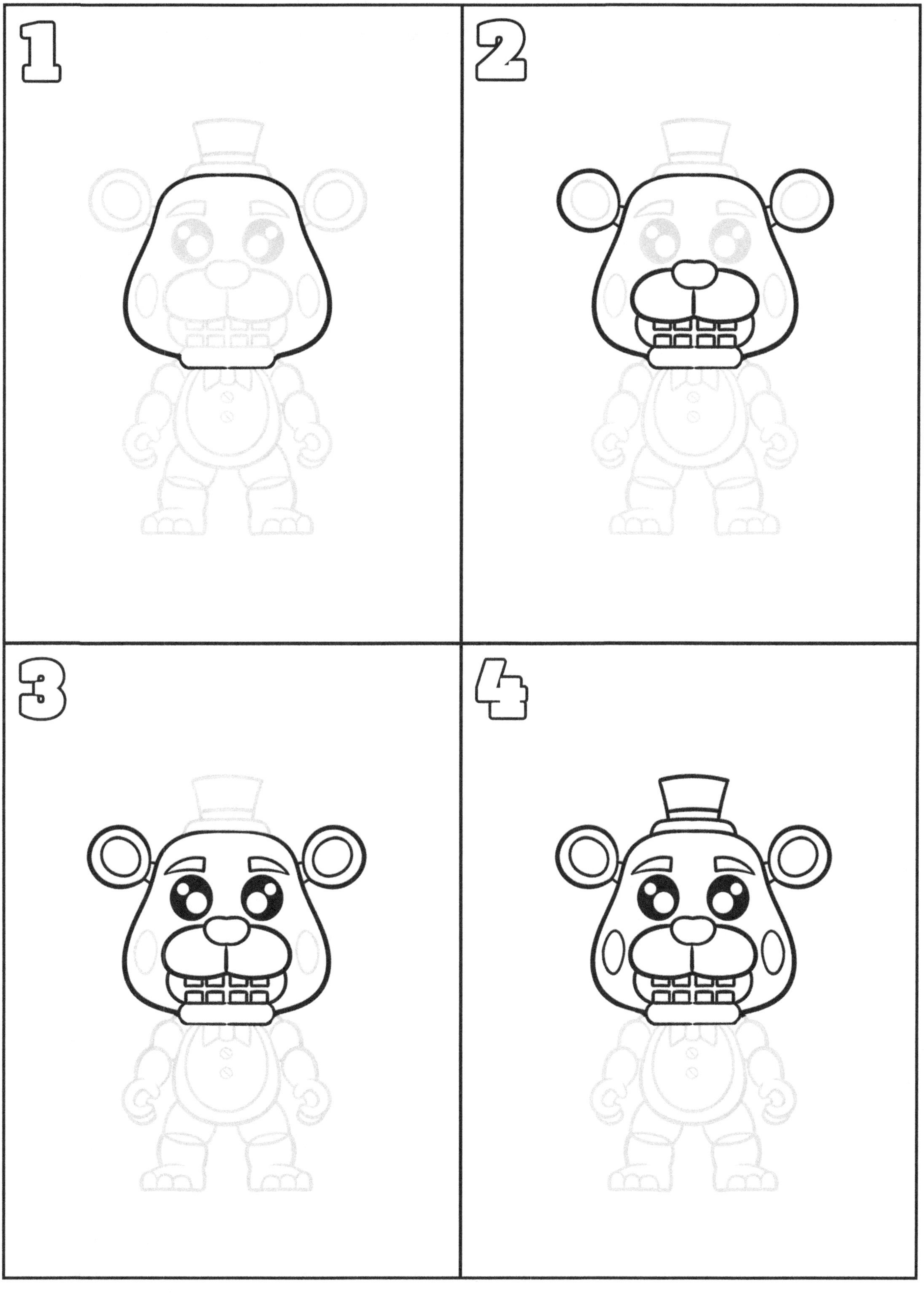
1
2
3
4

9

10

11

12

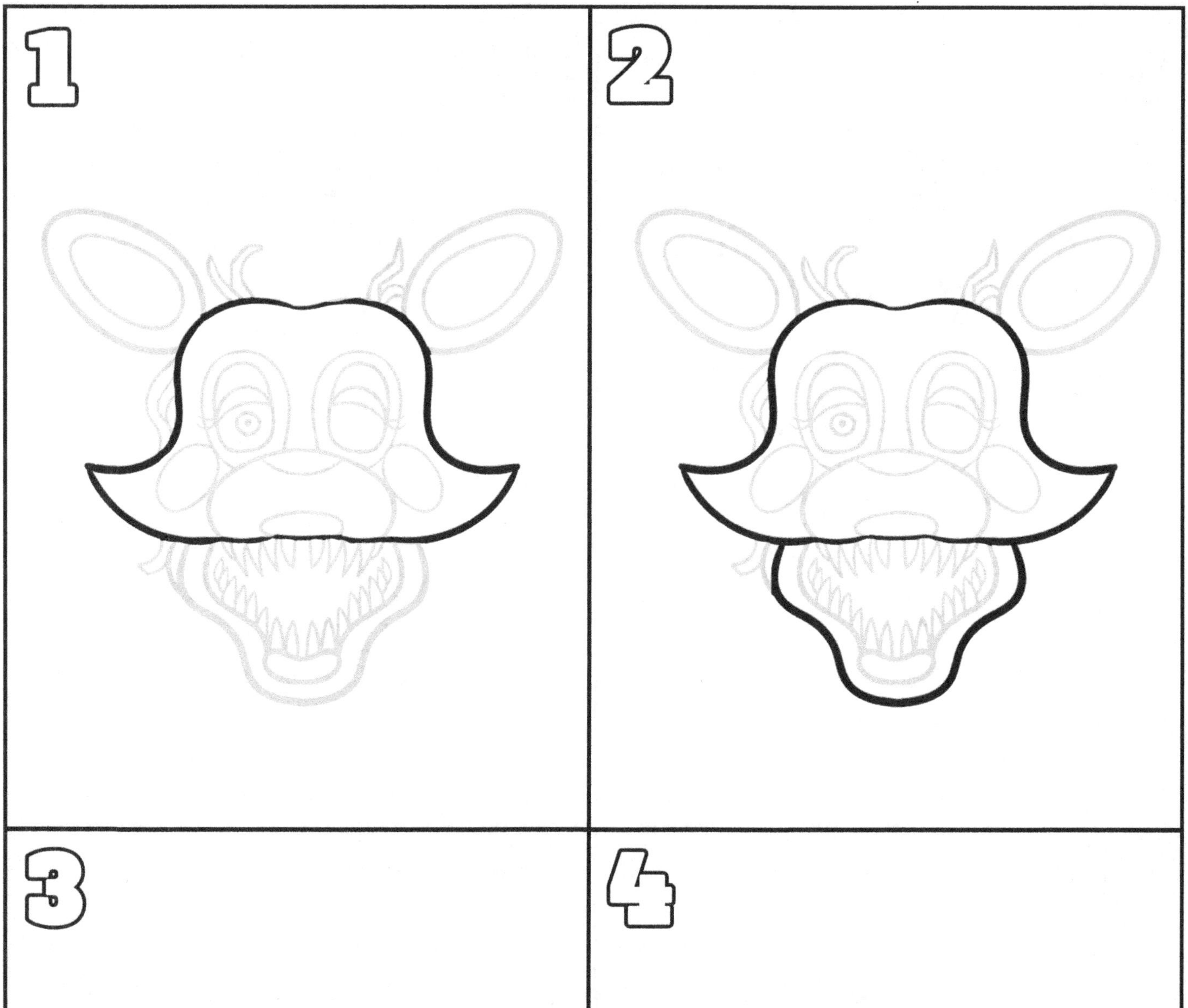
1
2
3
4

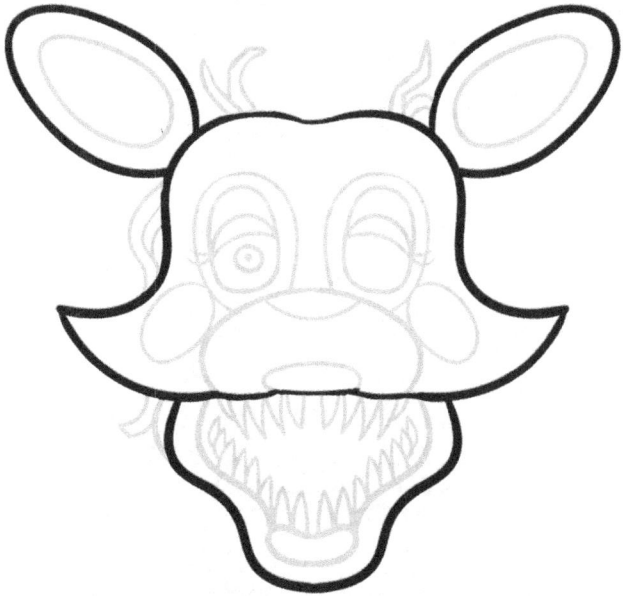

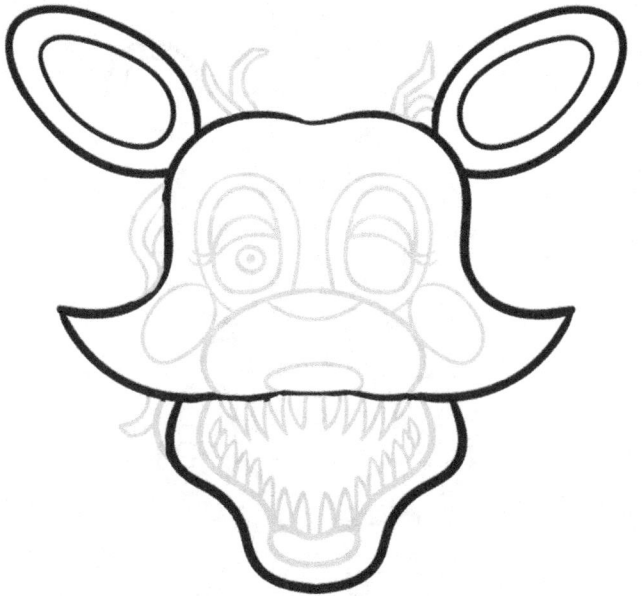

5

6

7

8

WRITE DOWN
WHAT YOU LIKE ABOUT THIS BOOK:

....

....

....

....

....

....

....

....

....

....

....

THANK YOU VERY MUCH
FOR TRUSTING AND CHOOSING
OUR PRODUCT

WISH YOU ALL THE BEST
IN YOUR FUTURE

HOPE YOU WILL PUT YOUR TRUST
IN OUR NEXT PRODUCT

Made in the USA
Las Vegas, NV
14 December 2023